9 BD

9th District Burglary Detail

A POLICEMAN'S STORY

Autobiography By Robert Porter

PAGE PUBLISHING, INC.
Conneaut Lake, PA

First originally published by Page Publishing 2021

ISBN 978-1-6624-3887-5 (pbk)
ISBN 978-1-6624-5244-4 (hc)
ISBN 978-1-6624-3888-2 (digital)

Printed in the United States of America

Law enforcement officers are never off duty. They are dedicated public servants who are sworn to protect public safety at any time and place that the peace if threatened. They need all the help they can get.

—Barbara Boxer

The duties of an officer are the safety, honor, and welfare of your country first; the honor, welfare, and comfort of the men in your command second; and the officer's own ease, comfort, and safety last.

—George S. Patton

ACKNOWLEDGMENT

Lt. Joseph Philban, Philadelphia Mounted Police, Ret.

Sgt. Robert Hurst, Philadelphia Police Dept., Stakeout Unit, Ret.

Very special thanks to my wife, Teri, for her hard work reading my "scribble!"

Special thanks to Ms. Lee Stevens, who helped me in getting this book started.

Thanks to Daniel Johnson for his help in putting the data into the computer and Rafael Odessay for his artwork.

INTRODUCTION

What Is a Police Officer?

A police officer is someone who protects and serves their community—continuously working changing shifts and leaving family and loved ones at home. A police officer puts on a uniform and goes to work every day with the knowledge that they may not be returning home to their loved ones at the end of their shift. They risk their lives every day just doing their job.

A Police Officer comes into contact with all sorts of people—people of different ages, races, ethnic backgrounds—people of different social and economic circumstances. They interact with people seeking safety from criminals and with criminals committing all types of crimes.

The changing shiftwork and the need to work every day of the year mean that officers are often not home to watch their children open their Christmas presents, and more often than not, they miss their children's activities such as sports, school plays, and musicals. There are also birthdays and bedtimes, as well as many other holidays and family celebrations that police officers have to miss.

On top of the difficult schedule, an officer can find it hard to forget the details of the day. They may bring the stress of the job home with them, which can be difficult for the family. While officers may keep most things about the job to themselves, especially the bad things they see, it can still cause the family to worry. A police officer's spouse is a special person because they know how difficult things can be. Being married to a police officer requires that they accept the danger and the stress involved in their spouse's job and do their best to enjoy the times they have together as a family.

I served as a police officer for the Philadelphia Police Department from 1969 to 1992. Within that time, my partner Peter Forjohn and I spent thirteen years as plainclothes policemen on burglary detail in the Ninth District of the City of Philadelphia. This area, encompassing Center City and the surrounding area, was packed in those early days with all kinds of businesses and people, which also meant all kinds of crime. In our first twenty-seven months on the job, starting in September 1971, we made a record 204 arrests, 149 of which were felonies. We received twenty-one commendations for our work, and the number of arrests and convictions we accomplished led to the creation of a citywide plainclothes unit called ACT-1 and ACT-2.

When I started working for the Philadelphia Police Department in 1969, it was rated one of the best in the country, with a force of eight thousand officers. Today, that number has been reduced to about 6,400. During my tenure as a police officer, the city experienced turmoil and violence reflective of those times.

When I retired in 1992, much in the department had changed, but the blue still ran deep in my veins. In this book, I tell the story of what it was like to serve as an officer of the law protecting the citizens of Philadelphia from 1969 to 1992, and within that, how my partner and I worked together in the Ninth District so successfully. While we received many accolades for our work, it was our dedication to helping others that really mattered and still matters to this day. Back then, because there were many more police on the streets of Philadelphia than there are today, when you called 911, the response would be quick and the investigation of your complaint thorough. But beyond that, we truly cared about helping those we were pledged to serve, and we were dedicated to keeping our city safe.

During my twenty-three years in the Philadelphia Police Department, and my partner's, Officer Forjohn's, thirty years, thirteen of which were spent on the Ninth District Burglary Detail, we never once had a citizen's complaint filed against us after 1,500 arrests, with a 98 percent conviction rate. On the contrary, while on the Burglary Detail, we received over forty-five letters that were sent to the Philadelphia mayor and police commissioner from citizens of Philadelphia thanking us for apprehending criminals while in the process of committing their crimes against said citizens. These crimes included robbery, attempted rapes, burglaries, and other felony offenses. The following are several of the letters we received.

CITY OF PHILADELPHIA

POLICE DEPARTMENT
HEADQUARTERS, FRANKLIN SQUARE
PHILADELPHIA, PENNSYLVANIA 19106

JOSEPH F. O'NEILL
Commissioner

February 19, 1976

Allen D. Black, Attorney at Law
1845 Walnut Street, 23rd Floor
Philadelphia, Pa. 19103

Dear Counselor Black:

Thank you for commending Officers Robert M. Porter, John Pigko and Peter F. Forjohn for their apprehension of two burglary suspects who attempted to break into your neighbor's home, on January 19, 1976.

I am personally very proud of the members of our department, but it is especially gratifying when one of those we serve expresses satisfaction with their performance.

The officers concerned, as well as their Commanding Officer, will be informed of your kind words. A copy of your letter will become part of their personnel file.

Sincerely,

JOSEPH F. O'NEILL
Commissioner

JFO'N:mi

Note: Some names and details have been changed to protect identities.

1437 Boxwood Drive
Blackwood, N.J. 08012
September 3, 1975

Police Commissioner Joseph O'Neill
8th & Race Streets
Philadelphia, Pennsylvania 19107

Dear Commissioner O'Neill:

On August 7, 1975, at six o'clock P.M. in the vicinity of 22nd & Market Streets, I was pushed into my car and robbed.

The next day I learned that my unfortunate experience was one of several recent incidents in that immediate area, and that Officers Porter and Forjohn of the Ninth District Burglary Detail were assigned to the case.

My co-workers and I were greatly relieved and secure in knowing that the area was under surveilence.

On August 21, 1975, just two weeks later, I identified the suspect, whom I understand was apprehended within a very short period of time.

This letter is written to express my deep appreciation and thanks to Officers Porter and Forjohn for their conscientious efforts which were most successful.

Sincerely,

Barbara Yannessa

Barbara Yannessa

BY:jb

n cc Officer Robert M. Poter # 3026
         "   Peter E. Forjohn # 4140
                 9th

ROBERT PORTER

2601 Parkway - Apt. 948
Philadelphia, Pa. 19130
February 24, 1973

Police Commissioner Joseph O'Neill
8th and Race Streets
Philadelphia, Pennsylvania

Dear Sir:

It was recently my misfortune to have my automobile nearly stolen.
Had it not been for the alertness of Officer Porter of the Central
Detective Division, the car probably would have been taken.

I was encouraged to sign a complaint against those involved in the
attempted theft.   The experiences which ensued gave me renewed respect for the thankless task of the officer trying to protect the
people of Philadelphia.   Two days in court to appear against men
with horrendous records and the possibility of having to appear again
are rather discouraging.   However, the interest of Officer Porter
and Detective Lawton Connelly made my part in it somewhat easier.
These two men are gentlemen and truly dedicated to a job which is made
so much more difficult by public apathy, unconscionable lawyers, and
a lenient judiciary.

If Officer Porter and Detective Connelly are representative of the
Philadelphia Police Department, you and Mayor Rizzo can be justly
proud.

Yours truly,

Officer Porter,
This is a copy of a letter sent to your
commissioner. Thought you might like to see it.

Elizabeth F. Nelson

Michael J. Manchester, Vice Pres.

RAD-O-LITE OF PHILADELPHIA, INC.

Emergency Traffic Control Systems

and

Electronic Protective Systems

3200 N. 17th STREET

PHILADELPHIA, PA. 19140

BA 9-2500

August 26, 1972

Joseph F. O'Neill, Police Commissioner
Philadelphia Police Department
Police Administration Building
Philadelphia, Pennsylvania

Dear Sir:

Mr. and Mrs. Sam Davis, owners of the Shop-Well Food Market at 2221 South Street, Philadelphia, Pa. and their employees, Kay Woothers and Sam Brent, have asked me to express their gratitude to you and the police officers of the 9th Police District and the detectives of the Central Detective Division for the prompt police action taken on Thursday, August 24, 1972 when their store was held up by gunmen, who took Mr. Brent and Miss Woothers as human shields. The responding police officers exercised good judgment and tact and exposed themselves to personal danger and it was miraculous that no one was wounded.

The Davis's and their employees feel that you should be made aware of the commendable action taken by the members of your department in this serious situation in apprehending these dangerous criminals.

Very truly yours

Michael J. Manchester

Michael J. Manchester

MJM:cls

ROBERT PORTER

October 9, 1973.

Police Commissioner Joseph F. O'Neill
8th & Mace Streets
Philadelphia, Pa.

My dear Commissioner:

Permit me to thank you for the service rendered by two
members of your 9th District Burglary Detail, Officers
Peter Porjohn (4140) and Robert Porter (3028) in an
incident which could have had serious consequences for
Mrs. Le Fevre and me.

At about 9:30 in the evening of last August 1, a burglar
entered the kitchen of my house by ripping the screen and
releasing a catch on the screen door. He had armed himself
with knives taken from a rack in the kitchen and also with
an electric iron which had been standing on a counter. My
wife and I were chatting after dinner in the adjoining
dining room. Meantime, fortunately for us, these two
officers had been observing the culprit and were able to
apprehend him before he could carry out his design.

Upon acquaintance with the two officers, I can attest
that they were thoroughly professional, gentlemanly,
courteous and dedicated. I can also assure you,
Mr. Commissioner, that this neighborhood feels much more
secure and has increased high regard for your department
on account of your innovation of the Burglary Detail. It
is to be hoped that you will find it feasible to continue
this service in center city.

Thanking you again, and assuring you of my esteem and
regard, I am

                    Respectfully,

_____

P.S. The delay in sending this letter has been occasioned
by our extended absence from the city.

Loc.
408 S. 18TH ST

14

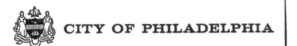

CITY OF PHILADELPHIA

DEPARTMENT OF PUBLIC HEALTH
COMMUNITY HEALTH SERVICES

Health Center #6
415 W. Girard Avenue
Philadelphia, Pa. 19123

LEWIS D. POLK, M.D.
Acting Health Commissioner

DAVID A. SORICELLI, D.D.S
Deputy Health Commissioner
for Community Health Services

February 9, 1979

Commanding Officer
Burglary Detail Division
9th Police District
20th & Pennsylvania Ave.
Philadelphia, Pa.

Re: Officer Pete Forjohn
Badge #4146
Officer Robert Porter
Badge #326

Dear Commanding Officer:

  I wish to express my thanks to the two police officers mentioned above
for their swift action leading to the capture of the two youths who had
assaulted me and grabbed my pocketbook on Wednesday afternoon, January 31,
1979, as I was walking in the subway concourse at the Lombard Street station.
The alertness and efficiency of the two policemen resulted in my getting my
pocketbook back in less than fifteen minutes after it had been grabbed.
(The incident occurred while I was returning from having attended a special
meeting at the main office of the City Health Department.)

  My thanks to Officer Forjohn for escorting me back to my car parked
at my office, Health Center #6, which by this time (5:30 p.m.) had closed.

  I am truly thankful and appreciative of the work of the officers mentioned
and to the other members of that unit. I wish them continued success and safety
as they continue to protect the people of this city.

Gratefully yours,

Ms Naomi G. Anderson

Naomi A. Anderson
Medical Social Worker
Health Districts #5 & 6

NAA/ma

Chapter 1

GROWING UP

The date was February 14, 1969—Valentine's Day. I had just been honorably discharged from the United States Marine Corps, having served three years on active duty—eighteen months of which were spent in Vietnam. I jumped into my 1963 Chevy Super Sport and headed home.

It would be an eight-hour drive from Camp Lejeune in North Carolina to my home in the Roxborough section of Philadelphia, Pennsylvania. The drive gave me time to reflect on my life and to think about the job waiting for me back home. I had previously taken the exam for the Philadelphia Police Department and had been accepted in the next class starting on July 7, 1969.

As I drove home, I thought about my years growing up. I was born on April 22, 1946, in a house on Coral Street in the Kensington section of Philadelphia. I was the fourth child of John and Ottilie Porter. My father was of Scottish, English, and Native American descent. My mother was German and Hungarian—one hell of a combination! The oldest of my siblings was John, named after my dad, then came a sister named Jackie, a brother named Harry, and then came me.

When I was five, tragedy struck our home. Our parents were grocery shopping, and my two brothers and I were playing cowboys and Indians in our small yard. Johnny was dressed in his cowboy outfit, and we had built a small campfire in the yard. Somehow, Johnny's outfit caught fire. My sister Jackie, along with my brother Harry, tried to put the fire out. But despite being taken to the hospital, Johnny passed away after a few days from severe burns.

I don't think my parents ever forgave themselves for going food shopping that day. After some time went by after Johnny died, my parents decided to move. They just couldn't live in that house anymore.

We ended up moving to a new section of homes in the Roxborough section of Philadelphia. They were nice single-family homes, each with a front and a backyard. The neighborhood, with about two hundred homes, was filled with young couples, and there were a lot of kids around the same age as we were. During the following years, my parents had three more children—my brother Donald and my sisters Marilyn and Doreen. So now there were six of us children!

Growing up in that neighborhood was a lot of fun—playing all kinds of games with the other children, and on Halloween, we were out for hours, filling up our bags with all kinds of goodies. Those were happy days.

Later on, as we got older, we guys in the neighborhood cut lawns and shoveled snow for the neighbors to make some money. Things were a little tough in those days for all of us. We even collected empty soda bottles to make money. At the time, the supermarkets gave 5¢ for a large glass soda bottle and 2¢ for a small one. When we had collected enough money, we would buy hot dogs and rolls, make a campfire in the woods that surrounded our neighborhood, and just have fun out there.

Growing Up

I even got a small paper route to make some money.

One day, as I was walking home from having delivered the papers, I saw my dad's car parked outside of a local bar called "Norman's." My parents always stopped there on Saturdays for a beer or two after having gone food shopping.

I thought I would stop in and maybe get a root beer and a meat-ball sandwich. Just as I was entering the bar, two police officers were escorting a male out of the bar.

I noticed that the male was bleeding about his nose and appeared to be intoxicated. Upon entering the bar, I saw my parents sitting on the barstools, and the owner of the bar seemed to be cleaning up broken glass from around the bar and on the floor.

I asked my parents what had happened, and they just sat there and said nothing.

Since bartenders were usually very knowledgeable on the "goings-on" at any given establishment, I decided to ask him what happened. This particular bartender happened to also be the owner. His name was Norman.

Norman told me that my parents had stopped in for a beer. There was also another guy sitting at the bar, and they engaged in a normal conversation. After a while, my dad went to the men's room. The male then decided to make a pass at my mother—who responded by punching him out! Norman then said the male fell to the floor, where my mother proceeded to kick him.

My father heard the racket and came from the bathroom just as my mother picked the man up from the floor and tried to throw him over the bar. It was then that Norman, the owner/bartender, called the police.

After that day, my dad decided to give my mother a nickname, one that only he could use for her, "Big Fella!"

After word got around the neighborhood, all my friends referred to my mom as "Big O." She was a tough lady that didn't put up with anything, yet she was also the kindest person you would want to meet. She was the lady in the neighborhood that everyone went to when they needed a babysitter.

We had a neighbor named Mike Jeskonis, who was a commit-teeman. He would stop by our home and talk to my parents about voting. Mr. Jeskonis had a Model T Ford truck, and during the win-ter, he would deliver coal to homes in Philadelphia. On Saturdays, I would help him, and he paid me fifty cents, which I would give to my parents. Having a large family and my dad changing from job to job made it difficult, so all of us kids chipped in to help out.

One spring, I got to play Little League Baseball for a well-known coach, John Boyce. He was such a great coach that they named a field after him, which is located at the corner of Henry and Roxborough Avenues. At the end of the baseball season, Mr. Boyce came to my house and told my parents that he wanted me to play in the Babe Ruth League. He told them I played very well, and he needed me on his team. My father told Mr. Boyce that I couldn't play because he got me a job selling produce for Mike Jeskonis during the summer. So every summer, from the time I was thirteen until I was sixteen, I sold produce from the back of a truck on the corner of Henry Avenue and Walnut Lane. I was just two blocks from the baseball field, and I could hear them playing, but family came first! I was paid $3 a day, which I gave to my parents. I did get a little pocket money, however, from the tips.

One night, after selling the produce, I got together with some neighborhood friends, one of whom had a car. We drove up to Tom Gola's Driving Range. It was on the corner of Ridge Avenue and Bells Mill Road. After we were finished and leaving, I saw a "help wanted" notice on the office door.

I asked the man inside about the sign. He told me they needed someone at night, from 6:00 p.m. until after closing at 11:00 p.m., to perform tasks such as picking up the golf balls that people hit and replacing the stock.

Now as we were hitting the golf balls, there was a jeep driving up and down the field, picking up the balls, and we were trying to hit the jeep with our golf shots. I guess that was the job I was applying for!

I asked the man what he needed from me, and he said I needed a driver's license. I had learned how to drive from my older brother Harry but didn't have a driver's license—I was only fifteen. I told him I didn't have it on me, but I was interested in the job. I went home that night and told my father, who handed me his driver's license. In those days, a driver's license only had a name and address on it, no date of birth or other information. So the next night, I went to the golf range and got the job. They always paid me in cash, and as far as they knew, my name was John Porter.

Four nights a week, I picked up golf balls from 6:00 p.m. until midnight. They closed at 11:00 p.m., but I had to have all the balls picked up and ready to go the next day. I hitchhiked a ride home. I gave 50 percent of my pay to my parents, but now I had some pocket money. I did this job until I was sixteen.

Following in the footsteps of my older brother Harry and my sister Jackie, I quit school at sixteen to go to work. My father got me a full-time job working for a man named Joe Charles. He owned Charles Rug Cleaning Company located at Ridge and Port Royal Avenues. I worked for him six days a week for $35 per week. My parents got $25, and I got $10.

Mr. Charles was an Armenian gentleman who, in addition to owning the rug cleaning business, also bought and sold used cars. When we finished cleaning rugs in the plant, he would have us clean the engines on the used cars he bought. After the car engines were cleaned, he would send them up to a property in upper Roxborough where he had a garage. The garage was on a large estate, where his mechanic worked on the cars. After the mechanic work was complete, the car would be taken back to the plant, where we would clean the interior, compound, and wax the auto to get ready for sale.

Besides the rug plant and used auto sales, Mr. Charles had a section of the plant set up as a thrift shop. He would go to Center City auction houses and buy lots of clothing, books, shoes, and other needed items. He, along with his brother Paul, would price the items, and on Fridays and Saturdays, he would open up the thrift shop for people to buy his goods. Like I said earlier, back in the 1950s and early 1960s, times were hard, and money was scarce. They kept the shop open from 10:00 a.m. to 8:00 p.m. every Friday and Saturday. Some weeks, I'd stay late to help them in the shop.

One night, just after they closed, I heard Joe and Paul arguing. Paul was complaining that they weren't making enough money on the stuff they sold. Joe said to Paul, "Am I losing money?" and Paul replied, "No, but you're not making money either." Joe's reply was "I'm happy we're breaking even. These families need the items we're selling." That's the kind of guy Joe was—he always cared for the other guy.

Joe Charles had a very large estate, which included a real mansion, grounds that consisted of many weeping willow trees, and the garage where his mechanic worked on the used cars to make sure they were in proper working order before they were sold. There was also a horse stable on the property that Mr. Charles leased out. One day, Joe asked me if I could work late and help his mechanic remove a transmission from a 1957 Plymouth. I said sure, and that's when I met his mechanic, Jerry Farmer, who would soon become my best friend for life.

Jerry Farmer worked during the day for a company that built fire trucks, and at night, when needed, he worked on Joe's cars. After a while, it seemed I was helping Jerry every night. When my day was over at the rug plant, I would meet Jerry at a diner called Land's Diner, which was only a block from the rug plant. We would get something to eat and then go to Joe's garage and work on the cars.

Sometimes, Jerry and I would work on the cars till the early morning hours, then we'd go outside and sleep on Joe's lawn. Joe would wake us up at 6:00 a.m., bringing us coffee and doughnuts. Jerry would then go to his day job, and I would go to mine at the rug plant. Many times when we worked at night, a police wagon from the Fifth Police District would stop by with coffee and check to see if we were okay—and we would shoot the breeze. Joe Charles was always good to the police, and in return, they checked on his property at night.

One Saturday, just as I finished work, Joe asked me if I could give Jerry a hand on Sunday. It seemed Joe had sold a car, and the buyer was scheduled to pick it up on Monday morning, but the transmission had to be replaced, and Jerry needed help getting the job done. I told Joe I couldn't help Jerry because I was taking a girl I knew to the amusement park in Willow Grove. He then said to me, "Are you sure? Jerry really needs your help."

I again told him I couldn't do it.

Early the next morning, there was a knock on the front door of my parents' house. The next thing I knew, my mother was yelling for me to come downstairs, that the cops were there. I had no idea what she was talking about.

When I dressed and went downstairs, the two officers started yelling at me and put handcuffs on me. These were the same cops— Joe Kelly and Bill Keys—who always stopped by the garage at night to check on Jerry and me.

They said I stole from a store the night before, and they were taking me to the police station. As my mother and father yelled at me and the neighbors stood waiting and watching outside, the two cops threw me in the back of the police wagon and took off. I kept telling them I didn't do anything, but they told me to shut up. They also told me they were ashamed of me and disappointed because they thought I was a good kid.

After riding around in the van for a while, it stopped then backed up. When the door opened, there stood Joe Charles and Jerry Farmer with big grins on their faces. Come to find out, my parents and neighbors were in on the whole thing. Needless to say, Jerry and I got the car ready for sale.

Between working for Joe Charles and Jerry Farmer, I had the best years of my life. Joe and Jerry were more like family and taught me honor and respect. They made a man out of me at the tender age of seventeen!

On Sundays, for extra money, I pumped gas at Bob Stuty Sunoco gas station, located at Ridge and Northwestern Avenues.

While working one day with Jerry in Joe's garage, we heard on the radio that the Gulf of Tonkin had been attacked by the North Vietnamese. Jerry looked at me and said, "You're going to war." My older brother Harry had recently joined the Marines and sold me his 1958 Chevy convertible, and Jerry had repainted it. I did get to use it for a while.

My parents would not let me enlist—I was only seventeen— but when I turned eighteen, I joined the Marine Corps for three years, due to report on February 15, 1966. My brother was sent to South Vietnam, stationed at Chulai. My parents got a little worried because his letters had stopped, but he was due to come home—his overseas tour was over in early February.

One night I was watching TV with my dad when my mother came out of the bedroom and asked my father if there was any beer in the fridge. My dad looked at my mother and said, "It's 10:30 p.m. You want a beer this late?"

She said, "No, Harry's coming home tonight."

My dad said, "Yes, there's beer in the fridge."

My mother went back to bed. My dad looked at me and shook his head. About ten minutes later, there was a knock at the door. It was my brother Harry. Our parents ended up having a welcome home party for Harry and a bon voyage party for me at the same time.

Once in Vietnam, I was an NCO with my own platoon. I didn't want to leave my guys, so I shipped over for another six months. I had been stationed in Phubai, South Vietnam, for thirteen months.

During the TET Offensive, both my sergeant—Carl Lowery—and Gunnery Sergeant, Gordon Hoover, were killed in action in Hue City.

When I left Vietnam for the flight home, we got word that Martin Luther King had been assassinated. What should have been an enjoyable flight home turned into a sad, depressing trip for all of us.

When I landed in California, I went to the airport desk and booked myself on an early flight to Philadelphia. I then called my mom and told her I would be arriving at the Philadelphia airport around 8:00 p.m. Because of my mother's sixth sense when my brother Harry came home, I decided to change my flight so I would arrive four hours earlier than previously scheduled.

Luckily, they had this flight available, and I was going to surprise my mother. Or so I thought!

While on the flight home, I met a young lady, and because I knew I'd have a few hours before my mom would actually arrive at the airport, I decided to ask this young lady to dinner, and she accepted. At the time, you still had to disembark from the plane the old-fashioned way—down the steps to the tarmac and then walk into the airport. As the young lady and I were walking up the steps, almost to the top, these two monster arms grabbed me and literally pulled me over the rail. It was my mother. I looked at the young lady, and she waved goodbye. My mom had gone to each gate that had a plane arriving from California. How embarrassing, but wonderful too! My mom (also known as Big O) had done it again.

As we pulled up to our house, there was a big sign on the lawn that said, "Welcome home." When I entered the house, in the corner of the living room was an artificial Christmas tree. I had missed two Christmases at home while I was in Vietnam. It was good to be home in Roxborough with my family again as I looked to the future and the start of my career as a policeman.

After Vietnam, I had three months before Police academy training would begin.

I spent time helping Joe Charles and my best friend, Jerry Farmer (working at Joe's Used Autos).

Joe then asked me if I would like a job taking care of eight (8) horses at the stable he had rented out on his property. The man who had previously been taking care of them retired. I immediately said yes, having been around those horses before I left for Vietnam.

One day, as I was tending the horses, one of the owners—who I had never met—a male, asked if I would cool off his horse and give him a rub down, that he was working late and had to leave.

I told him it would be my pleasure. About a week later, he came to the stable to take out his horse, and he asked me if I wanted to ride with him to Valley Green (a part of Fairmont Park). I said, "Of course." Exercising the horses was part of my job, so I saddled up ___ to Valley Green. It was then that he said, "By the way, my name is Teddy."

A week or so later, he was dropped off at the stable by a friend. After he went for a ride, he asked me if I could drive him to the Septa Bus Terminal, located at Ridge Avenue & Summit Street. I told him, "Sure".

Then we got to the terminal. There was a very large green bus there. He then took me onto the bus, where there were several other males sitting there. Teddy said to them, "This is the man that's been taking care of my horse."

The males sitting there on the bus were warm and friendly, and I noticed that a couple of them were holding guitars. It was then that I realized they were a band—musicians. The name of the group was Harold Melvin and the Blue Notes, featuring Teddy Pendergrass, and they were going on a tour. I did not see Teddy Pendergrass again until many years later.

After I retired from the police department, I opened up a Locksmith Shop in Lafayette Hill, Pennsylvania, at the age of forty-five. I was still single at the time. While in the police department and working burglary, I thought it smart not to get married due to the danger of the job. I dated but would not let it get too serious. While operating my locksmith business, I met and fell in love with a beautiful woman named Teri Stagliano. Teri was a customer service rep for a chemical company named Sartomer Inc., but on weekends, she sang in a band called Generation Gap. She had one hell of a voice and was classified as a professional. While we were dating, my girlfriend had a routine breast exam and was diagnosed with breast cancer. When I became fifty, we got married. After my wife's successful cancer treatment, we decided to go to a show at the Valley Forge Music Fair.

When we went to the show, they were selling raffle tickets. The prize was that they upgraded our seats and moved us upfront—first row, and after the show, we could meet the stars backstage. Well, to our surprise—they called our numbers, and we won!

Backstage, we met Roberta Flack, Peabo Bryson, Jeffrey Osborne, James Ingram, Patti Austin, and guess who—Teddy Pendergrass! Of course, I remembered Teddy right away, and he also remembered me! Although he was in a wheelchair, his spirit was high, and it showed in his performance. He was wonderful!

Chapter 2

BECOMING A POLICEMAN

The Physical

The written exam required for the Philadelphia Police Department was three hours long and held in a big room in a building in Center City with lots of other officer candidates. I can't say it was particularly hard, but I am not a test taker, so it took me more than one attempt to pass. Once I did, the next step was to report to the municipal service board in Center City for a complete physical. Little did I know how close I would come to failing the physical and walking away from a criminal justice career.

First, I met with a mental health professional who asked me a series of questions—that interview went well. Then I was examined by several doctors who also drew blood, gave me a hearing test and a chest x-ray. Last was the eye exam, administered by two doctors, a male and a female. I read all the eye charts with no problem. They checked my eyes with their scopes and found no problems there either. Then, when I thought I was almost done with the poking and prodding, they said there was one more test. It involved ten flip cards that each had different colored dots showing a number. I was doing fine until the last card. I could not see the number on the card, so the male doctor said I was color-blind and so had failed the eye exam and would not be able to become a policeman.

The female doctor then asked me a few questions about my military service in Vietnam. She said to the male doctor that I must have fifty-one reasons to pass this test. If my eyes were good enough for Vietnam, they should be good enough for the police department. The male doctor had me read the cards again. This time, when I got to the last card, I said the number fifty-one.

He said, "Okay, you passed."

I don't know if the male doctor saw the female doctor wink at me when she said I had fifty-one reasons to pass the test. My only regret is that I didn't get her name, so I was not able to thank her.

The Police Academy

July 7, 1969—my first day at the police academy! I arrived at 8:00 a.m. dressed in black pants, a white short-sleeved shirt, and a black tie, feeling a mix of nervousness, excitement, and anxiety. Each of us who was a new recruit was given a badge number and a payroll number. We were assigned seats in alphabetical order by our last names. Seated to the right of me was John Cannon, and to the left was Richard Schwiker. We were from the same neighborhood, so we drove to the police academy together, taking turns driving.

That first day was basic indoctrination, where we were given an overview of what the training would entail. Then the actual training began, covering the Pennsylvania penal code and the types and levels of crimes—for example, felonies are crimes that involve physical harm or largescale theft and fraud. They are part 1 crimes, while misdemeanors, such as petty theft or shoplifting, are part 2 crimes. We also learned about summary offenses, which in Pennsylvania are the most minor types of crimes. They include such crimes as disorderly conduct, loitering, harassment, and low-level retail theft.

Next, they taught us how to search or pat-down suspected criminals. One of the instructors—after being searched by us students—pulled out a gun that none of us had found while patting him down. We realized this was harder than it seemed, and after that, we practiced patting down a lot.

After a couple of weeks of classwork, we had driver's training. This was very important since we would need to know not only how to drive a patrol car but also, most importantly, how to maneuver it in challenging situations such as in pursuit of another automobile.

Then came the pistol range. We were issued Smith and Wesson 6-shot 38 revolvers and holsters then taken out to the pistol range. We were taught how to shoot but also the intricacies of when to shoot and when not to shoot. We were taught how to draw and fire our weapon, as well as how to shoot from all different distances from the target and from behind a fixed object.

After two months, our training was almost over, and we were sized for and issued our uniforms. Just before graduation, there was a riot at Holmesberg State Prison, and our class was called out there to assist in the crisis situation. We traveled by police bus, and once we arrived, our platoon was formed in the rear, and we were placed on standby.

As we stood in formation, the sergeant in charge of us introduced himself. His name was Jim Dolan, and his tone and demeanor made it obvious he didn't want to be in charge of a bunch of rookies. He told us he couldn't understand why he got this detail—watching over a bunch of rookie cops—while the action was going on inside the prison. We all felt really dumb, but then he asked if any of us was Irish. Several of the guys raised their hands, and he started to laugh.

We were there for about an hour—the whole time being told jokes by this sergeant who had changed his tune. In later years, I got to know him and discovered he was not only a great guy and a great joke teller but also an excellent banjo player. He belonged to one of Philadelphia's string bands that marched up Broad Street every New Year's Day in the Mummer's Day Parade.

Graduation Day

Finally, graduation day had arrived! Attending were some high-ranking officers, such as the Police Commissioner Frank Rizzo and city officials.

We were given our division assignments with orders to report the following Monday to the captain's office for our district assignments. To our surprise, Richard Schwiker, John Cannon, and I got the same district, which was the Ninth, located in Center City, Philadelphia.

We were told by some of the veteran officers that it was one of the best, most active districts in the city, meaning a lot of crime took place there and that we would never get bored working there. As we were dismissed for the weekend, we were told not to load our weapons until after we left the academy. I guess they didn't want any of us to accidentally shoot ourselves while still students of the academy!

Chapter 3

$\diamond$

SERVING THE PUBLIC AS AN OFFICER IN UNIFORM

While at the academy, we learned that there were several divisions within the police department—the central, south, north, west, and east divisions. Within each division, there were numbered districts. Central division, where I was sent, is consisted of the Sixth and Ninth Districts, and within those districts were boundaries of patrol. Central division covered Broad Street West to the Schuylkill River, north to Gerard Avenue, South to South Street. Connected to our division to the south was the south division, Seventeenth District. North of Poplar Street was the north division, which was the Twenty-Third District.

Each number on the patrol car indicated which division it was from and a number to which section the car and patrol wagon covered within their district. For example, on 917 car, which became mine, the number 9 was the district, and 17 was the section the patrol car covered. This section consisted of apartment buildings, homes, and businesses. It was an active patrol car.

First Day

When Richard Schwiker, John Cannon, and I reported to the Ninth District on our first Monday morning, the corporal in the operations room took us to meet the captain, whose name was Joe Rapone. We also met Inspector Chang. The captain assigned Richard Schwiker and me to the fourth squad and John Cannon to the third squad. Each district had four uniformed squads and one plain-clothes squad, which was called the fifth squad. We were each given a card with our work schedule on it. At that time, there were three shifts—8:00 a.m. to 4:00 p.m., 4:00 p.m. to 12:00 a.m., and 12:00 a.m. to 8:00 a.m. Within each squad, there was an A and a B section. Section A worked on the hour and section B on the half hour. This was done so that during a shift change—which took about twenty minutes—there would still be patrol cars on the street.

Each squad had one corporal. He controlled the operations office in that district. There were two sergeants—one was an upper-end supervisor, and the other was a lower-end supervisor. Plus, there was one lieutenant who oversaw the entire squad.

On our first day on the job, I rode around with the upper-end sergeant. I was learning the basics of patrol. I must say, this sergeant was a piece of work but knew the job! My friend rode with the lower-end sergeant.

Day work (8:00 a.m. to 4:00 p.m.) was somewhat busy, with calls about theft from shops—mostly in the area of Market Street and the lower end where there were a lot of businesses such as clothing stores, restaurants, and office buildings. I learned quickly that working the upper end, where it was mostly residential, was the best area to work with fewer radio calls.

Learning the Ropes as a Rookie

All of us rookies were on a three-month probation, so we weren't given our own patrol car until we demonstrated that we could do the job. Until then, I rode around with different officers—some from the upper end, some from the lower end.

I quickly learned there were a lot of different personalities in the department, and every officer seemed to handle a radio call differently. What I mean by this is that some officers mainly patrolled their sector and did the necessary bank checks, school crossings, store checks, and other routine jobs. Then there were the more active officers who made car stops, wrote tickets, and made arrests. But they all got the job done!

As rookie cops, we were also assigned walking beats in the district, usually on the lower end, in the business section of Center City. Once I had to stand guard on last out (12:00 a.m. to 8:00 a.m.) to make sure no one tried to drive across the Market Street Bridge due to a steel beam being loose overhead. It was a long night. Another night, working the same shift, I had to protect a woman in her apartment. I was not told who she was or why she needed protection. I was just told to sit inside the apartment while she slept in the bedroom and to make sure no one entered the apartment. Another night on that same shift, I had to sit in an apartment, where a homicide had been committed, to make sure the apartment remained untouched and no one entered it. But the one I disliked most was hospital detail. This involved sitting outside a hospital room for your whole tour to guard an individual—usually a prisoner who had been shot and arrested. Nothing ever happened, and I quickly ran out of reading material!

Robbery in Rittenhouse Square

Rittenhouse Square is a small historical park in Center City, with lots of trees and paths and park benches. A lot of pedestrians go to this park during their lunch hour and lounge on the benches, especially during warm weather. In fact, during the summer months, they lay on blankets and catch some sun during their break. In this environment, you'd be surprised at the number of thefts that occur—especially stolen pocketbooks—despite the presence of a uniformed officer who is stationed there every day.

The Philadelphia Mummer's Day Parade

For over 120 years, the Mummer's Day Parade was believed to be the oldest folk festival in the United States and has taken place every New Year's Day in Philadelphia. The parade consists of local clubs, usually called New Year's Associations, who compete in one of four categories.

1. The Comics

    Clowns in colorful outfits carrying multi-level umbrellas dance to recorded music, such as the Golden Slippers. Comics traditionally start the parade early in the morning, beginning in South Philadelphia and parading north up Broad Street to the city hall, where they are judged for prizes.

2. The Fancies "Golden Sunrise"

    This group, wearing fancy outfits, parades behind the Comics all the way to the city hall, where they are also judged.

3. The String Bands

    Approximately twelve different groups comprise this category. For a full year prior to New Year's Day, they work on their costumes, which are very colorful and must match the musical theme they have chosen. Although the group is judged at the city hall like the others, they also often stop along the way to play for thousands of spectators on both sides of Broad Street. The instruments consist of banjos, saxophones, accordions, acoustic guitars, clarinets, and more. At the same time, they also perform choreography, along with moveable props pertaining to their theme.

4. The Fancy Brigades

    This is the group with the most colorful and fancy outfits, and they are backed up with music as they perform to a musical theme.

The Mummer's Day Parade is truly a spectacle that lasts almost a full day. All the participating groups are volunteers who spend hundreds of hours over the course of a year putting their costumes together and perfecting their routines. But for the uniformed police officers working the detail, it is a long, usually very cold day spent watching the crowds for hours and making multiple arrests for pickpocketing and stealing pocketbooks.

Commander of the Central Division

Before getting my assigned patrol car, as I rode around with different patrol officers, they would talk about Chang, the Commander of the Central Division. He was an Asian man of medium build with a deadpan look on his face like he had no feelings. They warned me to watch out for him while on the 4:00 p.m. to 12:00 a.m. and 12:00 a.m. to 8:00 a.m. shifts. They all said Chang liked to patrol the district during those times and try to catch officers napping in their patrol cars. At least once every tour, our sergeant would call for a meeting, where he would sign our patrol log. He would also advise us to be on the lookout for Chang. I am proud to say, though, that during my time in uniform, while Chang was our commander, he never had to discipline any officers for their behavior during those shifts.

There were also the 8:00 a.m. to 4:00 p.m. daywork inspections by Chang. During the morning roll call, after the sergeant would inspect us and give out orders of the day, Chang would himself inspect the squad. We would stand at attention. He would then tell us to unholster our weapons, at which time we would point the weapons at the ceiling from a bent elbow. Then, as he approached, he would have each officer turn his pistol to the left and to the right to see if the weapon was loaded. According to Chang, some officers would forget to load their pistols.

He would then pick one officer and ask for his handcuffs. He would put his fingers in the chosen handcuffs and rotate them to see if they operated smoothly. He told us to keep our handcuffs in smooth, easy-operating service, slightly oiled for easier operation.

One week, while we were on daywork, we were informed by our sergeant that we were going to be inspected by Chang again. Leave it to the officers in my squad to do the right thing. We all went down to the locker room and oiled our handcuffs. Maybe we used a little too much oil.

Inspector Chang's uniform of the day was always a white shirt and black tie, while our uniforms were gray shirts. After Chang checked our pistols, he asked, as usual, one of the officers for his handcuffs. He then put his finger in the handcuffs and rotated to see if they were in smooth-operating order. Needless to say, his white shirt was splattered with oil. His only comment was "too much oil."

I was told by the veteran officers that one night, Chang called for an assist officer, and nobody responded. I don't know if that is true, but I can see it happening that way.

Assist Officer

When a call comes in over the police radio for an assist officer, all patrol cars race to help the officer with lights blazing and sirens blasting. *Assist officer* means an officer is in trouble, and you get to the officer as fast as possible, not stopping at red lights.

One call came in, and I raced to that location. Doing so, I went through a red light and hit the right rear corner of another patrol car that was also heading to the assist. While no one was hurt, as a rookie cop, I sure heard about it!

Uniform Patrol

After the three-month probation period, riding with experienced officers, I was given my first patrol car. It was number 919. That auto covered the smallest sector of the Ninth District, an area of about four-square city blocks. It covered Broad Street to Sixteenth and Poplar to Fairmont Streets. It was a racially mixed area, with both Black and White residents, but it was very quiet. I made some car stops, some pedestrian stops—routine police work.

After about a month in the 919 car, they gave me my permanent car—number 917. I guess they thought I was ready to patrol a larger and more active sector since 917 covered Twenty-fifth Street West to Twenty-ninth and Pennsylvania Avenue to Girard Avenue, plus Spring Garden Street. The neighborhood was mostly White residential. There were also two large apartment complexes at 2401 and 2601 Pennsylvania Avenue, both with large parking lots in front-facing Pennsylvania Avenue.

On day work—7:30 a.m. to 3:30 p.m.—my first assignment every weekday was to cover a school crossing for the little ones who were waiting for the school bus. That was at the corner of Pennsylvania Avenue, the windiest spot in the district and very cold in the winter. The rest of the day, I spent checking all the businesses on Spring Garden Street, which included checking and signing a logbook in several banks. Unless I received a call from police radio, that was the routine. I did, however, manage to make a few drug arrests and car stops. On the 4:00 p.m. to 12:00 a.m. and 12:00 a.m. to 8:00 a.m. shifts, there was always more activity. When making a car stop during those shifts, I would inform police radio of the location of the stop, and another uniformed patrol car would call police radio and inform them that they were backing me up.

Most of those car stops, I was backed up by number 911 car—Officer Peter Forjohn—since his sector connected to mine. Officer Forjohn was considered one of the most active officers in the district. Each patrol officer has a patrol log to fill out every day. On that log, we wrote the tour of duty and the date. All activity would be recorded on this log (radio call, car stop, arrests, security checks, etc.). Some patrol logs showed more activity than others, depending upon the activity within that sector. Some sectors are quieter than others. I came to notice that Pete Forjohn's log was almost always full on both sides. There were about fifteen lines to fill out on each side, which meant that he reported at least thirty activities for his shift.

In my sector, I got to know people, including the bad guys, especially two groups of brothers who had drug problems and criminal records. They got to know me too. Through my time on the 917 car, I arrested them several times.

The busiest time for the 917 car was 4:00 p.m. to 12:00 a.m. and 12:00 a.m. to 8:00 a.m. shifts. During these periods, I made numerous arrests for theft from auto, including stolen automobiles, burglary arrests, and robbery arrests.

During the summer of 1971, the City of Philadelphia Trash Collectors went on strike. When that happened, we had to work twelve-hour shifts to keep the city safe and calm. People were very concerned about disease. This went on until the strike was over—which made it very difficult for the police force and their families, as well as for the citizens.

Some of the calls I got while working the 917 car were somewhat odd—like one of the busiest days to be working the 4:00 p.m. to 12:00 a.m. shift—Halloween! One Halloween, October of 1970, I had several strange calls, such as the one to check out three nuns acting in a suspicious manner at Twenty-third and Spring Garden Street. I checked out the whole area and couldn't find the nuns. I called the police radio and informed them that there were none in the area. I got a laugh from the police radio and put myself back in service.

Shortly after that, I got a call to the 800 block of Twenty-sixth Street to meet a complainant who stated he was robbed of his Halloween candy. I went to that location and found a twelve-year old black male, who told me that four adult black males had taken his candy and run across Girard Avenue.

I put the description over the police radio. First of all, it was odd to see a black male in this area since this was predominantly a white neighborhood. I asked him where he lived, and he advised me that he lived on the other side of Girard Avenue, which was the Twenty-Third District. I then informed police radio of this information.

I then asked the young boy why he was trick-or-treating in the Ninth-District—a mostly white neighborhood. He told me that all the kids in this neighborhood were getting robbed of their candy, so he thought it might be safer to try the white neighborhood. I called police radio and asked them to keep me out of service so I could take this young man around to some of the homes to replenish his candy supply. Police radio said it was okay, so for the next thirty minutes, we went up and down Twenty-Sixth, Twenty-Seventh, and Twenty-Eighth Streets. By the end, his bag was once again full! I then asked police radio to have a Twenty-Third District patrol car meet me at the district's border to pick up the young man and see that he made it home safely. The Twenty-Third District officer was happy to help!

One night, from 4:00 p.m. to 12:00 a.m., just about the time my shift was over, I spotted a Black man on a horse at the intersection of Spring Garden Street and Pennsylvania Avenue. The horse looked like it was confused and walking in different directions. Upon taking a closer look, I noticed that the male riding the horse was "asleep in the saddle." The horse then walked to a grassy section of Pennsylvania Avenue and stood there. I got out of my patrol car and walked slowly toward the horse.

I tapped the male on the leg, and he woke up. I asked him if he was okay. It was then that I noticed he was intoxicated. I explained to him that the horse was wandering all around and that there was automobile traffic in the area. He told me that his horse knows the way home. I then told him to dismount and asked him for some identification. He said, "I'm going for my gun." I grabbed him and retrieved from his pocket a small automatic pistol. I placed handcuffs on him and called for a patrol wagon to take him in.

The man was very polite and apologized to me, that he was so drunk he didn't even realize I was a police officer. In his saddlebags were cans of beer. Apparently, he was out for a ride and some drinking, and the gun was for his protection. The patrol wagon arrived, and he was placed in it. I asked one of the officers in the wagon if he would drive my patrol car to the district. I then mounted the man's horse and rode it into the police district station. Being familiar with horses from my younger days was a privilege. Needless to say, there were a lot of funny things said about me that night. Mounted police were notified, and the horse was taken back to its stable. The man was arrested for carrying a firearm without a permit. At the trial, I explained to the judge how cooperative the defendant was upon his arrest and that he just had too much to drink. Because he had no prior arrests, he was placed in the ARD program, which is for first-time offenders when the crime is minor. If the male has no more arrests within a designated time (usually six months), his record is expunged.

While police radio calls can be for any number of reasons, the most serious calls were domestic abuse calls, hospital cases, suicides or attempted suicides (which mostly occur during the holiday season), rapes, assaults, and gang fights. Of all these, domestic abuse calls were the most hazardous for the police officers, and most always required police back up in order to respond. Domestic abuse can encompass many scenarios—husband and wife, parents and children, boyfriends and girlfriends. For the police officers answering these calls, it was usually always a no-win situation. Most often, if one or the other complainant is arrested, the abused complainant drops the charges.

Hospital cases are mostly minor, and the complainant is transported to a hospital. The more serious hospital cases are handled by the Philadelphia Fire Department Rescue Team. This rescue team would also cover mental health patients needing transportation to a mental health facility.

When receiving a call for rape or an attempted rape, a description of the perpetrator would be put out over the police radio and the complainant taken to the hospital. The case would then be turned over to the Sex Crimes Unit.

When an assault occurs, the complainant must first be treated for his or her injuries—if any—at the hospital, along with getting a description of the perpetrator.

In the upper end of the Fairmont section of the city, there were gang fights between two groups living in the area. We were called numerous times to break up those fights.

After about a year of riding the 917 car, some new recruits arrived at the Ninth District. Every day during the next three tours, I was given a recruit to ride with me so he could learn the job. Now I understood how the veteran officer felt when I was a rookie cop.

Between 1969 and 1970, I became very comfortable with my job. I made good arrests, and I was always active in my sector. My patrol logbook reflected my level of activity, as it was almost always filled on both sides.

Because both Officer Forjohn and I had full logbooks after most tours, our captain, whenever possible, placed us in a two-man patrol car on the 4:00 p.m. to 12:00 a.m. and 12:00 a.m. to 8:00 a.m. shifts. We worked the 911 car together, and we covered Pete's sector, along with my old car's sector. During late 1970–into early 1971, Pete and I made a fair number of arrests, and our patrol log was always filled out on both sides at the end of our tours.

During early July 1971, Pete went on Army Reserve duty for two weeks. I was back on my old patrol car, number 917, while Pete was away. One night while working the 12:00 a.m. to 8:00 a.m. shift, I had dropped off some paperwork at the district at 2:00 a.m. I left district headquarters and was driving down Callow Hill Street on my way back to my sector when I observed a station wagon go through a stop sign and make a right turn. I also noticed there was a taillight out, so I decided to make a traffic violation stop and pulled him over. Whenever I would pull over a car for a violation, I never had the intent to issue a citation unless they were driving in a dangerous manner. I called the police radio to inform them I was making a car stop and let them know the location. I was backed up by another officer from the Ninth District. I asked the driver for his driver's license and registration and informed him why I was stopping him. He gave me his license and registration, but the registration didn't match the automobile. He told me he was driving home from South Carolina, and he was in a hurry and very tired and apologized for going through the stop sign. I looked in the back seat of the station wagon and noticed a spare tire and jack. I asked him if he had had a flat, and he said no. I also noticed a glass jug on the floor in the back, which contained a yellow liquid substance. I asked him what the jug contained, and he told me it was urine. He told me he just wanted to get home, and he hadn't stopped anywhere. I then asked him to step out of the vehicle just as my backup arrived. I ran a check on the vehicle license tag, and it came back negative. I approached the driver to give him back his license. He handed me a $100 bill as he asked me if he could go.

Because the registration didn't match the vehicle, I asked him to open the back of the station wagon. He then begged both the other officer and me to let him go and offered us both more money to let him leave. We had him open the rear gate of his station wagon, and we noticed a large tarp covering the whole rear of the cabin. We lifted the tarp and discovered approximately fifty gallons of White Lightning or bootleg liquor. We then placed him under arrest and requested a patrol wagon to transport him to the Ninth District and had the recorder of the patrol wagon drive the car into the district station. We also informed the police radio of what we found in the station wagon. When we arrived at the district, we were met by both my sergeant and my lieutenant. They told me it was a great arrest. They had me, along with the officer who backed me up, put the 50 gallons of White Lightning in the captain's office. I made out a property receipt for the item, along with the arrest report, and went back out on patrol.

I noticed, however, that everyone gave me the cold shoulder whenever I stopped at headquarters during the rest of my tour. At that time, speakeasies were very popular due to Pennsylvania's blue laws that kept bars from being open on Sunday. The next morning, I hung around the district headquarters because I had court that day. When the captain arrived, he asked to see me in his office. When I sat down with him, he asked if I knew anything about White Lightning. I told him I knew very little—only that it was illegal. He then poured a little bit of the booze into his ashtray and lit it. It burned pure blue. The captain told me it was the best White Lightning he had ever seen. He congratulated me on the arrest. He then handed me a property receipt to sign for the illegal alcohol. I told him I had already signed for it the night before. He asked me to sign for it again, only this time the receipt said twenty-five gallons instead of fifty gallons. I wasn't born yesterday, so I gladly signed for the twenty-five gallons. Come to find out later that there was a wagon crew who had a tip about this stuff coming in, and they were waiting for it.

Problem was they had been called by police radio and were out of service when I made the car stop. I figured I messed things up for all parties concerned but was grateful my captain knew it hadn't been intentional on my part.

Chapter 4

<hr/>

ASSIGNMENT TO THE NINTH DISTRICT BURGLARY DETAIL

Pete and I continued to be the only two-man patrol car from 4:00 p.m. to 12:00 a.m. and 12:00 a.m. to 8:00 a.m. for another two months. After which, Captain Rapone called us in his office and asked if we'd be interested in working the burglary detail. We were told we would be in plain clothes and using our own autos, for which we would be getting 150 gallons of gas each month. Both Pete and I knew little about burglary detail. I had never heard of it, and though Pete had heard of it, he knew nothing about it. Despite our lack of knowledge, we gladly accepted and were on that detail for thirteen years.

The first auto I had was a 1964 white Chevy. Pete had a 1972 Plymouth Fury. When we started our first day on the burglary detail, we decided to switch cars every other day, as we would ride together. Problem was Pete's auto was light blue, the same as the patrol cars, so he had his car repainted. When he showed up in his newly painted Plymouth, it was now yellow with a black top. The only problem was that it now looked like the car from the TV show *Starsky and Hutch*!

Every day, working the 10:00 a.m. to 6:00 p.m. shift, we would check in with the captain and pick up the part 1 sheet. We would then drive to Nineteenth and Pine Streets to our first stop at a luncheonette called Towne Pizza, owned by a wonderful Greek family.

We made it our informal second headquarters as we always stopped there for coffee and for lunch. Towne Pizza had a standing rule for police officers—they never charged for coffee or soda, and lunch was always $2!

Our first stop of the day was at Towne Pizza for coffee and doughnuts. If Pete was driving, I would get us a cup of coffee and one doughnut each. We'd always pay for the doughnut. If I was driving, Pete would go in and get two cups of coffee and one doughnut. He would then split the doughnut and give me half. We would then pick a spot to park and go over the part 1 sheet as we drank our coffee and planned our day of roaming the streets.

Many times, one of us would drive while the other would walk the streets. We stayed in constant contact with each other via police walkie-talkie—the only option in the days before cell phones or pagers. If we felt we were on to something and our tour was up, we would stay on our own time. Often it paid off with an arrest.

September 13, 1971

On our first day on the burglary detail, Pete and I had a court case in Norristown for a guy we locked up in Philadelphia for stealing a car. He was also wanted in Norristown for a robbery. We contacted our captain and informed him where we were. He told us we could start our tour when we got back from court.

We arrived back at the district about 1:00 p.m., so our tour started at 2:00 p.m. and lasted until 10:00 p.m. We took two walkie-talkie radios and picked up the part 1 sheets, which were lists of crimes committed in our district.

The walkie-talkie radios had several bands on them. We put ours on the central band, which was our district. When we were following someone or got separated, we put them on the private band, so only the two of us could communicate with each other.

Around 6:00 p.m. on the first night, we observed a male hanging around a construction trailer in the 2,000 block of Ludlow Street. We then saw him break into the trailer. We waited for him to come out, and when he did, he had in his possession two power drills and a power saw. We then approached him, identified ourselves, and placed him under arrest. We switched our radio to the central band, identified ourselves as 9 BD, and requested a patrol wagon to come and transport the male to central detectives for booking.

September 14, 1971

In the area of Twenty-second and Parktown Place, an apartment complex, we noticed three males lurking in the parking lot. I knew one of the males from a prior arrest I made while I was in uniform.

After only a short time, we observed them break into a car and take things from the vehicle. We approached the males and made an arrest. All three were charged with burglary from auto, receiving stolen property, and conspiracy.

September 17, 1971

While in the area of Manning Street, around 9:00 p.m., we observed a male loitering and acting in a suspicious manner. When he saw us following him, he took off running. We apprehended him and then identified ourselves as police. He was taken to central detectives for investigation, where he was charged with loitering and prowling. He also had a police record for three prior burglaries. We later learned, through further arrests, that the father and son of the defendant were also criminals, with charges ranging from burglary to robbery to simple theft—a regular crime wave within the family!

September 21, 1971

While working the area of Fifteenth and Chestnut Streets, we observed two White males walking back and forth and looking all around while looking into every parked car they passed. Pete and I took up a surveillance of these males for several blocks. After a while, they started to separate, so we decided to stop them and take them to the Ninth District headquarters for investigation. Both males had in their possession a screwdriver and a coat hanger, tools that are widely used for breaking into autos. In addition, both men had police records. They were charged with possession of burglary tools.

September 28, 1971

While Pete and I were patrolling in the area of 2000 Ranstead Street, we heard a male screaming and observed a White male trying to rob money from another male. As we approached and I identified us as police, the White male took off running. After a scuffle, he was placed under arrest. He was then taken by patrol wagon to CDD, and the complainant was taken to CDD by us.

In our first ten working days on the burglary detail, we made six arrests with all the perpetrators charged and found guilty of the crimes.

We changed our working tours Monday through Friday—one day working the 10:00 a.m. to 6:00 p.m. shift and the next day, the 2:00 p.m. to 10:00 p.m. shift. This way, we could cover both the day shift and the night shift, as per the crimes being committed in the district and the part 1 sheet (crimes reported daily).

Looking the Part

As the days passed, Pete and I figured we should start looking, and sometimes acting, the part of the bad guys. Pete grew a goatee, and I let my hair grow long. I also grew a mustache and a beard. Later, when my hair got longer, I had my hair style changed to an Afro. At the time, that was the style for both White and Black, as well as Puerto Rican males. We also dressed the part in order to look less like cops.

One night in October 1971, Pete and I were working in the area of Seventeenth and Addison Streets, the southern end of the district. We were sitting in our vehicle, just observing when we were approached by males who asked us if we were interested in buying some cameras. We asked them how much and what type. They said the cameras were brand-new Nikons. We asked again how much, and they said $50. We told them we would buy them if they were indeed new. One of the men then asked for the $50. We told him we would give him the money, but he would have to stay with us while the other male said he would get the cameras. The one male then got into our auto while the other male said he would get the cameras. Pete was behind the wheel of the car, so I got out and had the male sit in front next to Pete while I got in the back. We then gave the male $50 in cash.

After about fifteen minutes of waiting, the male who was supposed to be getting the cameras hadn't shown up, and the male in the front seat tried to get out of the vehicle. I reached over from the back seat and held the male while Pete placed handcuffs on him.

We had information on two males who were flimflamming people in the area, and these two matched the description, so when they approached us, we knew what they were up to. We arrested the other male, who was hiding around the corner, and both were taken to CDD division. Both had bench warrants (wanted by police) for fraud. In fact, they each had over twenty prior arrests for fraud.

After the Arrests

After each arrest is made, the defendant(s) had to appear at a hearing in the Ninth District, where we testified to the arrest. The defendant(s) either had a public defender or a private attorney (if they could afford one). The defendants, through their own testimony, were then either held for trial or dismissed by the judge. We never had any defendant dismissed by the judge. They were all held for trial.

When their trial came up in the city hall, we testified before the court. Over 95 percent of the defendants we arrested in thirteen years on the job were found guilty of the charges. Many times, on the recommendation of their lawyer, they pleaded guilty before we even testified.

The upper end of the Ninth District (the Fairmount section) was mostly Puerto Rican. We made a lot of arrests for robbery, burglary, and stolen autos in that area. It got to the point where the district would get calls from the neighborhood, and they'd ask if Starsky and Hutch were working that day!

July 1972

Officers Forjohn, Mormello, and I were patrolling the area of Eighteenth and Rodman Streets when we heard screaming. We observed a male robbing another male. We placed one of the males under arrest and transported him to central detectives.

Our Record

From the beginning of working the Ninth District Burglary Detail, on September 13, 1971, to January 7, 1973, we made 130 arrests, of which 93 were part 1 felony arrests, with a 97 percent conviction rate.

By this time, Pete and I really looked the part of the street person, with long hair and beards. We really dressed the part!

One day, while at court in the city hall, I was sitting and waiting for my case to be called. There was a very well-dressed man sitting next to me. We were watching a trial that was going on. The defendant was answering questions from his defense lawyer. The well-dressed man next to me said, "If that was my client, I would have had him prepped for that question and had him answer it differently. He then would have received a not guilty charge." That told me that this man sitting next to me was a defense lawyer. It was very obvious to me that this man did not know I was a cop. I remained quiet, and we both continued to listen to the testimony. When that trial was over, they called my defendant's case. My defendant was brought into the courtroom from a holding cell, and he and his defense attorney sat down at the table before the court.

The court then called for Officer Porter, the arresting officer, to come forward and be sworn in. That was when the defense attorney sitting next to me, who had been giving me advice during the previous trial, realized I was a cop!

Just after I gave the oath on the Bible, I was ready to testify. The defense attorney stood up, asking to approach the bench along with the presiding district attorney. After a short talk with the judge, an agreement between the district attorney and the defense attorney was reached, and the defendant pleaded guilty to the charges. I didn't have to testify at all! As I walked out of the courtroom, the defendant's lawyer walked up to me and said, "Well done, Officer." Several years later, that very same lawyer wound up being a very prominent lawyer for the mob! I learned a little more about defense testimony that day.

Frank Rizzo and the Mounted Patrol

In January 1972, Frank Rizzo became mayor of Philadelphia. Prior to that, he was a police commissioner.

Frank Rizzo wanted to expand the Mounted Patrol of the city streets. The fifty-four men who were in the Fairmount Park Mounted Police were switched over to the Philadelphia Police Department. They were given uniforms and assigned park and city status, and Captain Charles Turner was selected as commander of the unit. The new training headquarters was on Northwestern Avenue in Chestnut Hill. The new training staff was led by Lieutenant George Smith. The trainers were Bob Casselli, Ted Cody, Bill James, Earl James, Rick Levin, and Dick Zelner. They were to train all new horses and fifteen new recruits for a ten-week period. Bill James was selected to model for a statue at the PAB holding a young boy.

In 1975, Lieutenant Smith was transferred, and Sergeant Joe Philbin was assigned as the new head of the training staff. Captain Turner was promoted to the rank of inspector.

In June 1978, the unit had 140 men, making Philadelphia the largest and best-mounted patrol in the USA! They also trained mounted officers from Wilmington, Delaware, Camden County, New Jersey, Valley Forge, Pennsylvania, and Kentucky, Texas.

The mounted patrol was assigned for crowd control at the following events:

- Flyers—Stanley Cup 1974
- Flyers—Stanley Cup 1975
- Phillies—World Series 1980
- All the New Year's Day Mummers Parades

All the mounted officers from Philadelphia were brought in every winter for one week of retraining. Mounted team and individual competitions were held each year from May until November. The trainers and a sergeant represented Philadelphia. Other entrants were the US Park Police, the Pennsylvania State Police, Wilmington, and Jersey City. Philadelphia won as the best team at the Devon Horse Show six years in a row, from 1976 to 1981. The individual rider trophy had to be won three times by the same team at Devon. It was called the McDevitt Trophy and was won by Sergeant Philbin in 1979 for Philadelphia. In addition, we had a twenty-four-horse drill team, which performed at the annual Thrill Show at JFK Stadium and for several shows at the Spectrum in Philadelphia.

When William Green was elected mayor in 1980, he cut the unit down by sixty horses due to budgetary reasons, and eighty remained. Horses were eliminated yearly until 2004 when the unit was disbanded. It was started up again in 2010, and they now have twelve mounted men on duty.

Philadelphia Police Department Stakeout Unit

I would be remiss if I did not mention the Philadelphia Police Department's Stakeout Unit, a newly formed unit of the police department, and one member of that elite group of police officers named Robert S. Hurst.

At the time, many crimes against insurance agents were on the rampage. As an insurance agent just before joining the police department in 1967, his experience made him the perfect decoy. He was also a decoy for the granny squad, which involved getting dressed as an elderly woman, combating crimes against elderly women, which were also on the rampage.

During his career, Bob was hospitalized over fifty times while in the line of duty, mugged 278 times, and stabbed eight times—once in the neck, paralyzing him for five hours. Fortunately, Bob suffered no major adverse injuries during his law enforcement career.

Bob was the recipient of numerous citations, commendations, and awards, both from the city of Philadelphia and the Philadelphia Police Department for valor, bravery, heroism, and merit. Making 1,600 arrests while functioning as a decoy, combating violent crime, he was known as the city's toughest cop.

Doubting Ourselves

During a period of time in January 1973, Pete and I did not make any arrests. The daily crime reports were still coming in, but we seemed to always be at the wrong place at the wrong time. Every week that went by without an arrest, the inspector, whose name was Kirk, would put up a finger. After he put up three fingers, we thought our job might be in trouble.

Fortunately, during the fourth week, we made five part 1 arrests then several weeks later, another four arrests. Our best week came several months later when we made a total of eight arrests, four of which were for robberies and weapon offenses.

Detail Assignments from Inspector Kirk

- April 26, 1973—Pete and I were assigned to a detail to Fifteenth and JFK Plaza (Love Park) to investigate complaints of females being harassed by a group of males during their lunch hour.
- April 27, 1973—it rained all day, so there was no activity at the park.
- April 28 and 29, 1973—there was no activity due to it being a weekend.

- April 30, 1973—Pete and I set up surveillance. What I did was lay on the sidewalk just across from Love Park. I had a coloring book and crayons, and I acted like I was coloring in the book. I tried to give the impression that I was "not all there." People walking by were giving me funny looks, but that was the idea. I also had a pair of opera glasses (small binoculars), so I could get a closer look at Love Park and the people there. Pete was parked in his car just outside the plaza.

Around lunchtime, the small park got crowded with mostly females who ate their lunch on benches surrounding the park. It didn't take long before a group of young males was observed harassing the females. I could see the females get up from their benches with their lunches and move away from the males. I radioed Pete, and we moved in and approached the group of males. We identified ourselves as police and called for a patrol wagon to take them to the police district. Record checks on these males showed minor prior offenses, and there were no warrants out for them. The group was warned not to return to the park to harass the women again. Pete and I continued to periodically check Love Park with no further problems.

A New Captain

We were told by the captain's office that there would be a new captain in charge of the Ninth District. Our old captain was transferred to the west division. We asked the clerk, Laura, what we should do because we were assigned to the burglary detail by the captain who was just transferred. The clerk told us to show up Monday morning and to identify ourselves to the new captain, Captain Ansel.

Now, a little about Laura, the civilian clerk who worked in the captain's office. She had been working in that office long before we got there, and she knew the ropes. She was a real sweet lady, not to mention very smart. We got to know her pretty well since being assigned to the burglary detail. She also knew how serious Pete and

I were about the burglary detail, along with my sometimes-juvenile antics—like coming in early and sleeping on top of the filing cabinets until she got there at 8:30 a.m.

Laura told us that the new captain was a very serious man and very strict with command. Pete looked at me, and I said, "Well, it was a nice ride." At exactly 9:00 a.m., the new captain walked into the clerk's office and introduced himself to Laura and the uniformed police clerk. He asked the uniformed officer to get him a cup of coffee from the operation room—cream, no sugar. He then walked into his office and closed the door. He didn't even look at Pete and me. I asked Laura what we should do, and she said, "Go out on the street."

The next day, Pete and I were back in the clerk's office, waiting for Captain Ansel. At exactly 9:00 a.m., he walked in, said good morning to Laura and the uniformed officer, who responded by saying, "Coffee, Captain—cream, no sugar."

The captain said thank you, went into his office, and closed the door. We were sure that Laura had told the captain who we were. The uniformed clerk got the captain his coffee, knocked on his door, and entered his office. A few seconds later, the captain came out of his office, looked at Pete and me, and then asked if we belonged to him. We said, "Yes, sir. We are your burglary detail." He then told us to bring our records into his office. We pulled our arrest files, knocked on his door, and entered his office. We explained to him when we were assigned and what we did. We also showed him our arrest records and assured him we would work for him only. He had never heard of a burglary detail but told us to continue what we were doing, and if he needed us, he would call for us.

After a few weeks passed and we made more arrests, he called us to his office. He said that our old captain started a burglary detail and would like us to go to his division and show his men how we worked the unit. We spent a few hours with the west division to give them a few pointers and hints as to working the burglary detail.

Requests from Captain Ansel (Not Pertaining to Police Work)

There were three times when Captain Ansel asked Pete and me to do him a favor.

The first time was early July 1973. The captain was having a Fourth of July picnic at his home, so he called Pete and me and asked us to go to a certain bakery in South Philadelphia and pick up a couple of dozen assorted rolls. He insisted that these rolls not contain any "air bubbles," which was the specialty of this particular bakery. We thought it was strange at the time, the issue of air bubbles in rolls, only to learn that many bakeries' rolls *do* contain air bubbles, which remove the flavor, which the bakery explained to us when we picked up the rolls.

The second time was when the captain asked us if we knew anyone in the clothing business because he was looking for a new sport coat to replace the one he regularly wore. He always came to work wearing a tweed sport coat and a fedora, and underneath his sport coat was his police uniform. He kept his police jacket, plus hat, in his office but preferred to drive to work looking like a normal citizen (smart move!). I told him that a friend of mine named Herman Tuckman had a men's clothing store in Roxborough. I knew Herman from Summit Park East Apartments in the Roxborough section of Philadelphia, where I lived at the time.

The captain and I drove to Mr. Tuckman's store. He looked around at sport coats, and after a short time, he found exactly what he wanted. The sport coat he picked looked exactly like the one he was wearing, but it was new. He told me he had been unable to find this same exact sport coat anywhere in Center City. He was very grateful to Herman Tuckman for having exactly what he was looking for, and he refused to take the discount Herman offered him.

The third time Captain Ansel asked Pete and me to do him a favor was a little different. His daughter had just graduated from high school, and her senior prom was being held at the Bellevue-Stratford Hotel in Center City. He asked us to pick his daughter up at home in the northeast section of Philadelphia, take her to the hotel, and drop her off, and then we needed to pick her up when the prom was over and take her home.

We felt sorry for the young girl, but her father was very protective of her. She thanked us for picking her up and taking her home, at the same time apologizing to us for having to do this. We asked her if she had a good time at her graduation party, and she said it was great.

The Launch of Another Burglary Detail

By the end of 1973, we had made a total of 202 arrests, with 149 being part 1 felonies. At the beginning of December 1973, the captain called us into his office and told us not to make any arrests that month. It was a strange request, but it seemed that headquarters thought that a lot of our time was being spent in court, which cut back on our street time. In addition, we were accumulating too much overtime, and headquarters wanted us to clean up some court cases.

Both the captain and I, along with Forjohn, came up with the idea of another burglary detail in our district to work opposite hours of Pete and me. This would give the district two burglary details, and we'd be able to cover the district for twelve hours a day.

The captain asked us for some recommendations of uniformed officers in the district who we thought would be good for the job. Pete and I made several recommendations, and the captain submitted the idea of another burglary detail to the police commissioner, who approved the idea. The captain then picked two officers from the list we had given him. Our call signs were then changed from 9BD to 9BD1, which was Officer Forjohn and me, and 9BD2, which was the new team.

For the month of December 1973, we worked with the new team, showing them our routine, which they picked up quickly. When arrests were made, our names were not placed on the arrest reports. On New Year's Day 1974, both teams worked the parade along Broad Street, keeping busy arresting pickpockets along the parade route. It was a constant shuttle between the two teams—going back and forth to central detectives with the defendants for processing.

The working hours for both teams were laid out so that there was complete coverage of the Ninth District from 8:00 a.m. to 10:00 p.m. Monday through Friday (the busiest crime hours in the district). The schedule would be 9BD1 working one week on Monday, Wednesday, and Friday from 10:00 a.m. to 6:00 p.m. and Tuesday and Thursday from 2:00 p.m. to 10:00 p.m. The two teams would alternate their working hours every week, though there were times we would work together when the hours dictated and arrests were made.

Each team maintained its own filing cabinets in the clerk's office. After each arrest was made, Forjohn and I had copies of the defendant's photo ID, along with the charges they were arrested for. We also had our personal memos that were used to refresh our memories of each person.

When the report of a crime came in, with a description of the perpetrator and type of crime, we would go to the files if we thought it was someone we had arrested before. If we found one that seemed to match the description and the crime committed, we would notify central detectives, and they would then show a group of photos to the complainants to see if they could ID the perpetrator. Having these records on file often resulted in arrests.

Police Training Slides

In the fall of 1975, Captain Ansel called Pete and me to his office. He told me that the police administration building and photo lab wanted to make a training film for the police academy to show the police procedures for making an arrest.

The captain then said I would make a perfect suspect in an arrest because I already looked the part. Needless to say, I had no problem with that. A few days later, the photo team showed up at the district. They explained to me what they wanted to do for the training film. To make it as simple as possible, they wanted to show the actual crime being committed, as well as the procedure for the arrest and booking for that particular crime.

They decided that the crime would be an assault charge. The first picture they took was of me punching and assaulting a civilian, after which uniformed police showed up and arrested me. They showed me being patted down for weapons then being handcuffed and placed into a patrol wagon and taken to the Ninth District. They then showed me getting out of the wagon and taken to the operations room, where the paperwork for my arrest was handed to the corporal.

I was then taken upstairs to central detectives, where I was interviewed by the detectives about the assault and to determine what charges they would be bringing against me. After that, I was placed in a cell, waiting to be transported to the police administration building, fingerprinted, and sent before a judge. PS. They wouldn't let me out of the cell (just breaking my stones). I was then given a hearing date.

I was returned to the Ninth District, given my personal items, and after signing for them, I was released. It was an interesting opportunity, experiencing what it was like to be arrested. The only problem was that all the uniformed officers of the Ninth District seemed to enjoy seeing me in handcuffs. All fun-loving guys—so much for Hollywood!

ACT Teams

After a few years, around 1979, with arrests being made at a record pace by both burglary detail teams, the captain called us into his office and told both teams that we were doing a great job in the district. He added that the state of Pennsylvania had given the city a grant to start a whole unit of burglary teams that would patrol citywide. These new units would be called ACT1 and ACT2 (anti-crime 1 and anti-crime 2), and each team would consist of two plainclothes officers in an unmarked police car patrolling the city.

The captain then said that the new unit's commander had requested that 9BD1 and 9BD2 have first dibs at joining the new unit and sharing our knowledge and experiences with the new unit. We immediately declined the offer because we were very happy where we were. The captain said he was glad to hear it. Both 9BD1 and 9BD2 felt very comfortable, and we didn't want to lose the contacts and informants we had accumulated over the years.

We also knew that state-funded programs always come with conditions and are usually short-lived. And so it was with ACT1 and ACT2. One of my close friends and a fellow officer of the Ninth District joined the ACT teams, only to last a few months. He told us it was nothing like he thought it would be. He never had a regular partner and was never patrolling the same areas of the city, which made it difficult to develop contacts or establish informants, let alone make any arrests. He became so disappointed with the ACT teams that he requested a transfer back to uniform patrol in the Ninth District.

We of 9BD1 and 9BD2 only came in contact with the ACT teams a few times, when they would show up after we had made an arrest. They would hear a request from 9BD1 or 9BD2 from the central band over the police radio for a patrol wagon to transport prisoners, and then they would come to our location and ask if we needed assistance. We knew the officers of the ACT teams were dedicated to their work, but the unit, for whatever reason, didn't last too long. We do know that there was an investigation of all ACT1 and ACT2 and the district's burglary detail officers. Word came down from our captain's office that a female prostitute had put in a complaint about a plainclothes police officer from one of the units who had relations with her. The female complainant gave a description of the male as a White plainclothes cop.

So police headquarters had all White police officers from ACT1 and ACT2, along with burglary teams from center city, report to staff officers with the internal affairs unit for interviews. When you were called down to staff headquarters, you knew it was for a serious crime committed by police. 9BD1 and 9DB2 were called down to staff headquarters, one officer at a time. Officers from 9BD2 were called first. One officer went to staff, was asked some questions, and then returned to the Ninth District. Officer Forjohn and I and the officers from 9BD2 asked him what happened. He told us they put him in a room where the only light was coming from the sunlight streaming in through a window. He was told to have a seat and that someone would be in to talk to him shortly. He said he sat there alone for about twenty minutes. Then a staff officer came in, asked a few questions, and dismissed him.

The same routine was carried out with the other male from 9BD2 and again with my partner Pete. I was the last to be called. Being known for my antics, while waiting to be called, I went to my filing cabinet, where I kept a stash of Silly Putty eggs that I would sometimes carry with me for amusement purposes when on surveillance.

When I reported to staff, they put me in the same room, with the only light being what came in the windows. I was told to have a seat and that someone would be in to speak with me. After a few minutes, I got up from my chair, went to a corner of the room, and sat down on the floor. I took out my Silly Putty and started throwing it at the wall, trying to make it stick. After about fifteen minutes, a staff officer walked in, looked at me, and told me I could leave. He never asked me a single question.

The investigation by staff continued for the next several weeks, but the outcome was never known.

In November of that year, we got a new captain at the Ninth District. Our former captain, who we had for eight years, was promoted to staff inspection. He was then sent to staff headquarters, where he decided to retire. He had been hoping for a division to command but didn't get it.

Our new captain, Captain Murray, was a good commander. He was also a member of the Kensington String Band that performed in the New Year's parade. On New Year's Eve, the day before the parade, our captain said to both BD teams that he would be in the front row of the parade and for us to look for him. Usually, on New Year's Day, our assignment was to cover the groups along Broad Street to watch and arrest pickpockets, who were always present during the parade.

New Year's morning, as both teams 9BD1 and 9BD2 were heading to the parade, the captain in charge of ACT1 and ACT2 informed us that he was in charge of all plainclothes units for that day. We informed him of our yearly assignments along the parade route. He told us his men from ACT1 and ACT2 would be covering the parade, and he had another assignment for us. He then had us sit in the area of Logan Circle for the entire day. Logan Circle is six blocks from Broad Street, where our captain would be performing in the parade. We never got to see him perform, let alone do our job arresting pickpockets. We never heard over police radio any arrests being made by ACT1 and ACT2.

The next morning, both teams—9BD1 and 9BD2—reported to the captain's office. He and the Kensington String Band had come in the first place, which is a big honor. He had a big grin on his face and asked us how we liked the string band. We told him we never got to see it and explained what had happened. He immediately got on the phone with the commander of ACT1 and ACT2. Needless to say, our captain laid into him, telling him he would never again be in command of his burglary teams. If it hadn't been for his burglary teams, there would never have been an ACT1 and ACT2. We felt that the captain of ACT1 and ACT2 was maybe angry at us because we turned down his request that we transfer to his unit, and this was his way of getting even with us. After that, we couldn't recall seeing any ACT1 or ACT2 teams in the central division.

Busting a Social Security Purse Snatching Scheme

Pete and I were working the 2:00 p.m. to 10:00 p.m. shift in early December. We stopped at the operations office—as we did every day—to pick up a part 1 sheet (a list of crimes committed during the past twenty-four hours). We got our walkie-talkies and then hit the streets!

As usual, we picked up our coffee at Town Pizza and then picked out a spot to park and go over the part 1 sheet. We noticed that a robbery (purse snatch) had been committed in the 2000 block of Aspen Street in the prior early afternoon. We drove back to the district to get more information on this robbery because several months earlier, there was another purse snatch in this same area around the same time. After seeing this report, Pete and I patrolled that area for several days with no luck and no robberies reported.

As we were going over the part 1 sheets for the previous couple of months, we noticed that these robberies were happening only at the beginning of every month. That's when we realized the women were being robbed of their Social Security money. At that time, Social Security checks were mailed to recipients, who would then go to the bank to cash them.

We went to our captain and told him what we thought was happening and that we would pick up our detail of the area at the beginning of the next month. We interviewed several of the elderly female victims and learned that they would take a bus to their bank in Center City, cash their checks, and then return by bus, which would let them off on Aspen Street. They would then walk to their homes from there.

That's when I got the idea to dress as a woman at the beginning of the month and get on a bus from Center City, getting off on Aspen Street. I told Captain Ansel our idea. The captain, knowing I was always game for anything, agreed. We then contacted the stakeout unit to see if we could borrow their radios because they had better equipment than we did.

That was the first time I met Police Officer Bob Hurst. This man was a legend within the Philadelphia Police Department. I asked him for a few pointers about being in disguise, for he was a master at it.

When the time came, I borrowed my mother's housedress, nylon stockings, winter coat and hat, and finally, her makeup. I put on a pair of eyeglasses, and to hide my mustache, I wore a scarf around my face. I was the laughingstock of the district!

Pete dropped me off in Center City by a bank, where I observed several senior citizens cashing their Social Security checks. I walked out of the bank, counting my Michigan bankroll, and I put it in my purse then got on the bus that would take me to the area of Aspen Street. Pete followed in his car, and we kept in contact by radio. We did this three times without success. It looked like I got "dressed up" for nothing, but on the fourth time, it paid off!

That fourth time when I got on the bus, Pete clicked my radio twice to let me know that a male fitting the description of the purse snatcher also got on the bus. As I got off the bus at Twentieth and

Aspen Streets, so did the male. I started walking west on Aspen Street, as did the male. After about a block, Pete radioed me that the male was picking up speed and was about to grab me. The male then went for my purse and started running, continuing west on Aspen Street, where we apprehended him. He was charged with attempted robbery—purse snatching. He was taken to the juvenile division, where he also confessed to the other purse snatches in that area.

Although we stopped the purse snatches in that area, the crimes against senior citizen's Social Security money continued—but at a much larger scale. These crimes evolved into robberies by a gang of males, who Pete and I had previously arrested for kidnapping and robbery. The story of these males can be found in the chapter titled "Robberies."

Dressing as an Old Woman

So we kept getting reports
periodically, like once a month
or twice a month it would happen
So at this time I had an idea,
I gave my idea to Pete and we
took it into the Captain. And what
I did was I went home and I borrowed
my mothers dress, her scarf,
around her head, right? And her sneakers,
nylon stockings, went into the district
and I dressed up as a woman.

The only problem was I had a mustache.
But it was wintertime, So I put the scarf
around my face, with glasses. At the time
I didn't have glasses, but I put on glasses.
And the scarf over my head, and a wig.
And along with stake-out unit,
cause stake-out had the really good radios,
with the ear sensor, so you can listen,
we had the bigger ones.
We borrowed their radios,
and I got dressed up in the Captains office.
Came out and needless to say by the district
laughing at me, saying I'm a idiot,
but that's me.

Bob Hurst, legendary stakeout officer

Bob Hurst in 1980, as a police decoy in a Philadelphia alley hoping to attract "sharks," or thugs, who prey on "critters," or easy marks. Some called him the city's toughest cop.

Bomb Scare

Pete and I were involved in only one bomb scare. It was during the summer of 1975 when we responded to a radio call around noon of a possible bomb at one of the office buildings in the 1900 block of Market Street.

We arrived at the scene just as the pedestrians were being evacuated from the building. We informed police radio that we were on the scene and that we would check it out, just as uniformed officers arrived.

We then talked with the cleaning person—the individual who had found what he thought was a bomb. He took us up to the ninth floor and showed us the office where he said the "bomb" was located. We advised him to leave the building for his own safety.

We walked over to the desk and looked at the so-called bomb, only to see that it was a novelty clock made of plastic that looked like sticks of dynamite wrapped together. We immediately notified police radio of our findings and made the call as unfounded (no bomb). We really felt bad for the cleaning person who honestly thought it was a bomb. We told him he did the right thing by calling it in.

Move

In the early 1970s, a black cult, calling themselves *Move*, settled into a house in West Philadelphia. The house had no electricity or running water, and they believed in eating all their food raw. They caused many complaints from neighboring residents, but when the city tried to evict them, they armed themselves against the police.

The city was concerned for the health and safety of the many children who lived in the house. Mayor Rizzo did everything possible to solve the problem, but the male members of Move continued to defy the city.

In 1978, a confrontation occurred between Move and the police. Police were surrounding the house when all of a sudden, a shot rang out. A Philadelphia police officer was killed, and a small firefight ensued. After the confrontation, arrests were made, and the house was destroyed.

By 1983, Move again set up a new headquarters at 6221 Osage Avenue, which was a row home in the middle of the block. The Move members then turned it into a fortress. All their neighbors were begging the city to get rid of them. Because the Osage Avenue location was in a Black neighborhood, this was not considered to be a racial problem but a health and safety issue. Living conditions were deplorable, to say the least.

The city officials did their best to ease the situation, but Move members were adamant against negotiations and refused to leave. Plus, and very importantly, they were well armed with weapons. Despite repeated requests to vacate and complaints from all the neighbors, Move would not budge.

On May 13, the police commissioner demanded their surrender. As a result, shots rang out from fortified positions within the house, and a gun battle erupted.

Pete and I were advised to stay out of the area because we were in plain clothes, and we were told that only uniformed officers and stakeout units would be involved. We remember the police commander was calling for more ammunition—that's how bad it was!

Then came several hours of silence.

Mayor Wilson Goode, the first Black mayor of Philadelphia, had a very difficult choice to make—to call for a wrecking ball to knock down the house or to have a small explosive device dropped on it. Either way, it was a very difficult decision. All the neighbors were ordered to evacuate their homes and were given a couple of hours to comply.

At 5:00 p.m., Mayor Goode decided to use the explosive device. A satchel containing explosives was dropped by a helicopter. The roof immediately started to burn, and Move was advised by a loudspeaker to please vacate the premises. The fire spread to neighboring homes so fast that the fire department (who was already on the scene) could not bring it under control.

Some members of Move and their children did escape from the rear of the building and were rescued and brought to safety. Sadly, eleven residents (five being children) were killed in the fire. By the time it was over, sixty-one-row homes were completely destroyed. All adult Move members taken into custody received multiple charges, including murder and child endangerment.

Several days later, after the fire was out, Pete and I drove to the 6100 block of Osage Avenue. The neighborhood looked like something from the second World War. All the homes in that area looked like they had been bombed. The city hired a builder to rebuild the homes, but when the builder failed to meet the construction code, the homes had to be destroyed again and rebuilt, costing the city millions of dollars.

Pope John Paul II

Around the third week of September 1979, Captain Ansel called Pete and me into his office. He told us he wanted us to check every tall building in the area that overlooked Logan Circle, to check out any possible place where a sniper might position themself with a rifle and have a clean shot at the pope, who would be giving mass on Logan Circle.

Pete and I spent the following week recording possible sniper positions on paper. The Philadelphia Stakeout Unit was also checking for possible sniper positions and was well-positioned to protect the pope, but Pete and I were told to limit our survey to the immediate buildings around Logan Circle.

We gave our report to the captain about a week later. He then informed us that on the day of the pope's visit, we would have to be in uniform. It was all hands on deck. We realized we would have to get haircuts, and I would have to shave my beard. We also had to get our uniforms cleaned and pressed because we hadn't worn them in eight years!

On the day of the pope's arrival, October 3, 1979, we were advised by Captain Ansel that we would be walking next to the pope's limousine, Pete on one side and I on the other side. When the pope arrived, he was met by Mayor Frank Rizzo, who, upon meeting the pope, bent on one knee and kissed his rings in the presence of Cardinal John Krol.

After the ceremonies of greeting the pope, he gave mass the next morning at the cathedral of Saint Peter and Paul located at eighteenth and Ben Franklin Parkway. Pete and I stood by the pope's limousine, expecting him to enter it after mass, but the pope and his entire procession, which included over one hundred priests from around the country, walked one city block from the cathedral to Logan Circle, where a large platform and altar with a large cross had been constructed. From this spot, the pope would perform mass before the one million people who were gathered there. The weather was perfect, and there were people stretched into the distance as far as the eye could see.

After the mass, the pope entered his limousine and departed with city officials and his procession for lunch and other meetings. Pete and I remained by his limo until he retired for the night. The next morning, the pope went to the Philadelphia Civic Center for more meetings and breakfast. After all his activities were complete, it was time for the pope to leave. Pete and I stood by his limo until the caravan of automobiles, along with uniformed police vehicles, were set to leave for the airport.

Before the detail, Pete and I were told not to stare or try to speak to the pope, just to salute him when he entered his limo. The last time he entered the limo to leave for the airport, I looked at him just as it was pulling away and saw him wave at me as I was saluting him. I saw him look over at Pete's side of the limo and wave at him too. After the limo was gone, I said to Pete, "The pope waved at me."

Pete, being a Catholic, explained to me that he wasn't waving at us. He was blessing us. I've never felt that close to God. It was a very long two days of standing in one place, for hours at a time, but it was well worth it. For me, it was a historical and touching time.

Needless to say, the next day, I started growing my hair and my beard again.

International Drug Dealer/Homicide

It was the second week of July 1981. Pete was on military duty with the National Guard, so I teamed up with John Pisko from 9BD2 for the day.

We checked with Captain Ansel to see if there was anything special he wanted us to do. He gave us a picture of a White male, about twenty-five years of age, telling us he was an international drug dealer who was wanted for homicide in New Jersey. There was information that he was in the Center City area and possibly staying in one of the main hotels in that part of the city and that he had several passports. John Pisko and I immediately started checking all the hotels in our district.

Coming up blank on four of the known hotels that we thought would have someone on the run, we started checking the larger and better hotels in the Ninth District. We entered the Wyndham Hotel on Eighteenth and Parkway, showing the photo of the man to the desk clerk, who said he didn't recognize him. We decided to hang out for a few minutes anyway, knowing that the desk clerks are shift workers, and maybe a clerk from another shift would recognize the male.

Just then, a bellhop was walking by with a tray of drinks. We showed him the picture, and he said he recognized the male and that he was taking the drinks he was carrying out to the man, who was by the swimming pool. I asked the bellhop to give me the red vest he was wearing. I put it on and took the tray of drinks out to the pool with Officer Pisko a few steps behind me.

We noticed the male lying on a lounge chair in the company of a White female. After I gave the drinks to them, Officer Pisko and I identified ourselves as police. The male jumped up and went to a wall that was directly behind him. He was planning to jump, but then he realized that the pool area was three stories above the street. We handcuffed him and called for a patrol wagon to take him to central detectives.

The female with him had no idea who he was, having just met him at one of the nightclubs a few nights before. She was cleared and released by central detectives.

After a few weeks, Officer Pisko and I went to the Burlington, New Jersey, courthouse to testify about our arrests. It was the same courthouse where the famous Lindbergh trials were held. It was the easiest arrest we ever made. Our captain was very, very pleased.

Chapter 5

TALES FROM THE TRENCHES

Bank Robbery

During our thirteen years on the burglary detail, the team made only one bank robbery arrest. Pete and I had made arrests of several different males for part 1 offenses, only to find out later that there were warrants out on them for bank robberies! We only made one arrest of a male when the bank was actually robbed.

Pete and I, along with Officer Denbeck from 9BD2, responded to a call from police radio of a bank holdup at Thirteenth and Market Streets. We went to that location and spoke to the teller that helped us. She told us that it was a male who worked at John Wanamaker Department Store. She knew this because he had cashed his paycheck there regularly. This day, he had handed her his paycheck to be cashed along with a note that said to "give him all the money, this was a holdup, he had a gun."

We then went to Wanamaker's personnel office to get the personal information of this employee who had just robbed the bank using his paycheck. The man had not returned to the Wanamaker building, so we proceeded to get his name and home address.

We went to the apartment building where he was living and knocked on his apartment door. We got no response, so we set up a surveillance of the apartment by hanging out in the hallway just down from his apartment. After about twenty minutes, a male fitting his description came walking down the hall, carrying groceries and a six-pack of beer. As he put his key in the lock of his apartment, we identified ourselves as police. He opened the door of his apartment, telling us he "didn't have time to talk."

We proceeded to put handcuffs on him and pat him down for weapons, which he did not have. We retrieved the stolen money from the bank, which he had in his possession in his pocket. We then called for a patrol wagon, and the man was taken back to the bank, where he was positively identified by the teller as the man who robbed the bank. He was then transported to central detectives for processing.

Judges

As time passed and we were appearing in the courts numerous times, we got to know the judges well. We learned that if the defendant had a private attorney, the case could be continued—mainly because the attorney was judge shopping.

Private attorneys would have the case continued (or rescheduled) until they found a judge who would give their client a better judgment in the case. Sometimes, this happened because the judge was friends with the lawyer, and sometimes, it happened because the judge was known to be more lenient.

There was one judge who had a reputation for turning his back on the witnesses and officers giving their testimonies during the trial. This would continue through most of the cases. This judge would only face the court to ask the lawyers, witnesses, or police officers a question pertaining to the case. Then he would turn his back to the court until he received a decision.

There was another judge who refused to hear my partner Pete's and my testimony because neither of us was wearing a tie in court. Now you must understand, we were always in street clothes (plain clothes) to do our job. So to appear before this judge, Pete and I would carry a necktie in our pocket and would put it on to testify. It looked stupid, but it served its purpose. After a few months of that, the district attorney's office met with the judiciary, and the forcing of wearing neckties in the courts stopped.

Another judge—during his lunch break—would walk through Center City looking at construction sites (nice hobby)!

Then there were the judges, who at one time were either a district attorney or a public defender. When they became a judge, they had to judge strictly by the law. Some public defenders became tougher on the defendants while others did not. It got to the point when Pete and I walked into a courtroom, we knew how the case would turn out—even before testifying. A judge cannot look at a defendant's past police record until he or she is found guilty of the charges that were presented to the court. This would then have an affect on the sentencing by the judge. If the defendant was found not guilty, the judge would not look at the past police record.

There was one public defender that Pete and I came into contact with for a lot of cases, and we never lost a case to him. He eventually became a judge. There was one instance where his court was swamped with cases to be heard. When one case came up, he called both the public defender and the assistant district attorney to approach the bench. After a short conversation, the public defender and the assistant district attorney returned to the table. Our case was then called, and the defendant pleaded guilty—no need for us to testify.

According to the assistant district attorney, the judge asked the public defender how strong his case was. The judge told him he was swamped with cases, and he knew Pete and me and that he never won a case against us. The public defender and the assistant district attorney agreed to have the defendant plead guilty rather than waste the court's time on the defendant's weak case. Now that was something to see!

Another judge story started on December 23, 1980, at approximately 2:40 p.m., when we received information over police radio of an armed convicted felon who had just escaped from the sheriff's custody inside room 378 of the city hall by pulling a 357 pistol from his coat pocket and pointing it at the judge. He also put it in the face of Inspector Fensel, who was in the courtroom on another case. A description of the escaped prisoner was given to the police by Inspector Fensel.

Minutes later, Pete and I observed the suspect cross Market Street from Seventeenth Street. As Pete and I identified ourselves as police, the defendant pushed me and started running west on Market Street. It had snowed that morning, and the streets were icy. As the defendant was running, with me in pursuit, he started slipping on the sidewalk, at the same time reaching for the 357-magnum pistol from his rear pocket. I talked to him while reaching for the gun that was now halfway out of his pants.

I managed to grab the gun, and I threw it under a parked car as we wrestled on the sidewalk. During the short scuffle, I also took my own pistol from my belt and threw it under the car. Pete and I finally got control of the defendant and placed handcuffs on him and called for a patrol wagon to take him back to the courtroom at the city hall. Just after the arrest, I realized I had severe pain in my right thigh, probably from the original tackling of the male.

Pete and I returned to the courtroom along with the defendant. The male was taken before the judge he had previously pulled the gun on. The judge asked him if he was injured in any way, to which he stated, "No."

Inspector Fensel, knowing I was in pain, told the judge I was injured during the arrest. The judge looked at Inspector Fensel and at me and said, "I'm not interested in the officer's injury."

I then said, "With all due respect to the court, f——y——!" and proceeded to walk out the door. I thought my partner Pete was going to have a heart attack.

He said to me, "It's all over for us!" He thought I would be fired, and I told him I didn't care.

Inspector Fensel then said to us, "Don't worry. I've got you covered."

This judge was well known and disliked by many for his leniency toward convicted criminals. The defendant was charged with four counts of aggravated assault, threats, PA Uniform Firearms Act, and other related charges.

Dealing with the FBI

While working the 2:00 a.m. to 10:00 a.m. tour of duty, the 9BD responded to a call on Eighteenth Street of a possible burglary. When we arrived, along with uniform patrol, we entered the three-story brick home.

We were met by a woman who told us she thought someone had been in the home. My partner and I searched the property. Nothing seemed to be missing, but we had a strange feeling about the property and the woman. When we left the house, both Pete and I agreed that it looked like a mob safehouse—by the way, the rooms were made up.

About twenty minutes after we left, we received a call from Uniformed Patrol Car 93 for a meet. When we met with 93 Car, they told us the woman of the house wanted to talk to us privately. We returned to the house and met with the woman, who then asked us for help. She told us that she was the caretaker of the property and that it was used by people who came from out of town and that they would stay only a short time—sometimes just a couple of days. She said it was her job to see that they were taken care of. She then handed me a copy of a bearer bond in the amount of $50,000 signed by a well-known mob boss from Florida. The woman seemed very frightened and didn't know what to do.

The following morning, Pete and I took the copy of the bond to our captain, William Ansel, and told him everything that happened the night before. He looked at the copy of the bearer bond and then made some calls. Pete and I went back onto the street.

After about an hour, we were called into the captain's office. When we arrived, two FBI agents were already there. We told the FBI agents what had happened, and the agents asked us if we would follow up with the woman to try to get more information.

The captain and I decided that only I would contact the woman, keeping my partner Pete out of it—Pete being married and me being single. The captain felt it best—plus the fact that two people meeting with the woman would raise suspicion.

About a week or so later, I met the woman at the house for dinner. We made it look like we were friends, being she was also single and dating. It was then that she told me a shipment of counterfeit $50 bills would soon be coming up from Florida and that they were to meet a man from Pittsburgh who was going to buy the counterfeit bills. She didn't know at that time when the buy would take place.

She handed me one of the $50 counterfeit bills as proof of her story. Now at that time, there were no cell phones or even pagers, so we set up a place and time to be in contact with each other.

I then took the counterfeit bill to Captain Ansel, who called in the two FBI agents. When I told them about the meet with a man named Dale, who was to buy the counterfeit money, both the Captain and I were shocked at their lack of interest. They said they were more interested in the bearer bonds than the counterfeit money, but they promised they would pass the information on to the Pittsburgh office. All we could do now was to wait for information from the woman as to where and when the meet was to occur.

After a few days, when I met with the woman, she told me that the meeting and sale of the counterfeit money were going to take place on the coming Saturday on the Pennsylvania Turnpike outside of Pittsburgh, at a Howard Johnson's rest stop. She didn't know the exact time and place but thought she would know just before the buy. Again, we informed Captain Ansel, who in turn gave the information to the two FBI agents, who said they would forward it to the Pittsburgh office.

Orders were given to the Ninth District Operation Room that if a woman called and asked for me, they were to contact me by phone so I could pass the information on to the two FBI agents. I stayed at my home all night, waiting for a phone call that never came.

It seemed the woman did call the Ninth District, but whoever took the call didn't notify me. When I went to work Monday morning, there was a message left for me at the captain's office to call the federal building in Center City. When the captain came in, I told him about the message to call the federal building.

When I called the federal building, I was told I was to appear before a grand jury to testify about counterfeit bills. I was then informed by the agent that an arrest of sales of counterfeit $50 bills was made on the Pennsylvania Turnpike outside of a Howard Johnson rest stop, just outside of Pittsburgh. The arrest was made by an undercover FBI agent by the name of Dale.

The captain and I were furious over the screwup of the two FBI agents that we were in contact with because they never did contact the Pittsburgh FBI Office about the counterfeit information I had received—which in turn put the woman in a tight spot.

Now I had to testify at a grand jury hearing before all the defendants and at the same time try not to jackpot my informant without lying to the grand jury. During a break from the courtroom, I met with the FBI prosecuting attorney and told him it was an FBI screw up by the two agents I was in contact with and that they screwed everything up by not contacting the Pittsburgh FBI about the counterfeit bills, or it would have been handled differently, and my informant's life would not be in jeopardy. I didn't know what the outcome of the trial was because I was dismissed after my testimony, but a few weeks later, I bumped into the woman. She thanked me for all I did and told me that no charges were brought against her and that she no longer worked as a caretaker of the safehouse. After that, I never saw her again but heard she moved out of state.

That's the one and only time I dealt with the FBI—and never again! But I can still to this day hear my captain chewing out the two FBI agents who screwed everything up.

Chapter 6

---⟨∞⟩---

PURSE SNATCH/ROBBERY

A purse snatch is when someone forcibly takes a purse from a female. The following are just a few of the over two hundred arrests made for purse snatches from September 1971 to August 1983:

January 10, 1971

While I was on patrol at 10:30 a.m., I was stopped by a female, who told me her purse had been taken from her at Twenty-third and Aspen Streets, near the Eastern State Penitentiary. I got a description of the male from her and put this information over the police radio.

When I first arrived in the area, I didn't see anyone who fit the description she gave, so I started checking out the area, driving slowly around. Then at Twentieth and Poplar Streets, I observed a male who fit the description coming out of a small field. He noticed my patrol car and ducked down in the field. I pulled my patrol car around the corner and got out. I waited and watched the field, focusing on the spot where I last saw him. After a short while, he must have assumed I hadn't seen him, and he walked out of the field in my direction. When he got close enough, I placed him under arrest. He was then taken back to the scene of the purse snatch and positively identified by the complainant. Several weeks later, I was given my first commendation for merit at roll call for my persistence in making the arrest. I asked Pete Forjohn to pin the blue ribbon on my shirt above my badge. I felt really proud. Little did I know that day that during my career, I would get nineteen more commendations/letters.

While still a rookie, I received the following for fire rescue:

In recognition of your policework, you are officially commended in that on August 21, 1971, at 7:00 a.m., you and Sergeant Raffaele, along with Officers Steele, Reeves, and Russell, safely evacuated four persons from a flaming hotel located on Fifteenth and Naudain Streets.

Because of your commendable efforts in the performance of your duties, you have reflected credit on the entire police department. Notation of this commendation will appear in your personnel record.

September 12, 1973

While patrolling the area, Officer Forjohn and I observed a male snatch the purse of an elderly female. We gave pursuit and apprehended the male at 420 S. Carlisle Street.

September 27, 1974

Riding in the vicinity of Twentieth and Lombard Streets with Officer Dembek from 9BD2 around 5:00 p.m., a call came over the police radio, reporting that two juvenile males had just committed a purse snatch in the area. At Twenty-fourth and Manning Streets, we saw two males who fit the description of the thieves. We apprehended them and took them back to the scene of the crime, where they were positively identified by the complainant and then placed under arrest.

November 10, 1975

Officer Forjohn and I were in the lower end of the district (south street)—patrolling that area because of previous reports of several juvenile females robbing purses from pedestrians. After a few hours, we saw three females who fit the description and set up a surveillance of them.

After a short period of time, we observed the females attempt to take a purse from a woman. We then arrested the women, and they were taken to the Ninth District and turned over to juvenile division detectives.

April 27, 1976

While on patrol with my partner Officer Forjohn in the lower end of the Ninth District, we observed a male acting in a suspicious manner. He was constantly looking around and walking in different directions. We set up a surveillance of him with me on foot and Pete circling in the car. We kept a visual on him while communicating with each other on a private band on our walkie-talkies.

We followed the man for about an hour when he crossed Broad Street into the Sixth District. We kept up our surveillance despite the fact that he had left our district. When in the 1200 block of Locust Street, the man tried to forcibly steal a purse from a female. At that time, we arrested him.

December 14, 1977

While patrolling the lower end of the Ninth District around 8:30 p.m., we took up a surveillance of two men who were acting in a suspicious manner—walking up and down the street, stopping and looking at females as they passed, sometimes walking toward a female then stopping, only to return to their walking up and down the streets again.

Then the two men walked east on Delancey Street, crossing Broad Street into the Sixth District. We continued to follow them—Pete on foot while I drove the car. When the two men forcibly grabbed a female's pocketbook in the 800 block of Delancey Street, we immediately placed both of them under arrest.

Chapter 7

ROBBERIES AND ASSAULTS

Just a few of the over five hundred arrests made:

August 24, 1972

At 3:20 p.m., while working the Ninth District Burglary Detail, Officer Joe Mormello and I were in the area of Twenty-second and South Streets when we noticed four males walking into the supermarket at 2221 South Street. We noticed that they all had heavy coats on, despite the fact that it was summer, and one was wearing a wig.

Joe and I crisscrossed in front of the supermarket, casually looking inside. As we passed each other, I said to Joe, "Shotgun," and he said to me, "Sawed-off rifle." We then crossed the street and tried to contact police radio through our walkie-talkies, but we could not get through, so we decided the best plan of action was to wait until they came out in order to ensure the safety of the people inside. We tried again to get through to police radio without success, not realizing we were in a dead zone.

After a short while, two of the four men came out. One, his coat hanging over his left shoulder, headed north on Twenty-third Street, and I followed him, checking behind me for the other two males. Joe followed the other, who walked north on Twenty-second Street.

When the one I was following got far enough away from the supermarket, I snuck up behind him, put my gun to his head, and said, "Police! If you move, I will shoot you." I then told him to get on his knees then to lay flat facedown on the sidewalk. When he dropped to his knees, he dropped his coat, and the shotgun was exposed. I then placed handcuffs on him. At this time, two off-duty police officers who were in a bar across the street came over to assist me, and I explained to them what had happened. I again tried police radio, and this time, I got through. I informed them of the situation and told them to send a wagon to my location to get the prisoner and that I was returning to the supermarket because two males were still unaccounted for.

As I was rushing back to the supermarket, Officer Mormello called police radio—he had the second male in custody, plus another one who had the getaway car. Now we knew that five males were involved. I entered the supermarket and saw that all the citizens were ducking and lying on the floor. I identified myself to them and told them to stay in place. One man told me the holdup men had the manager in the back room and had a gun on him.

Uniformed officers started arriving at the scene. They saw the male holding the manager, point of gun. I told him to give up—that we already busted his friends. Just then uniformed police entered a rear door of the market. The male then dropped his gun, and he was placed under arrest. Next to him was a green trash bag full of cash. Fortunately, no shots were fired, and no one was hurt.

Addendum: Before the trial, one of the defendants was shot dead during *another* holdup.

November 23, 1973

Just after noon, while driving alone south on Twenty-third Street at Pine, an area where there had been numerous reports of a male robbing doctor's offices and stealing handbags, I observed a male carrying a brown trash bag. As he was crossing the street, he took several handbags from the trash bag. I parked my car, walked up to him, and identified myself as police. The male then ran south on

Twenty-second Street. After an extensive pursuit through local bars and shops, the male jumped a fence in the neighborhood. As I gave chase and hopped over the fence, I was struck by a rock on the head. I got up, blood streaming down my forehead as I saw the male jumping over the next fence. I then fired my revolver three times, striking him. As he jumped the fence, I continued to give chase. I heard a door crash open and a woman scream. I entered the property and observed the suspect limping up the steps of the home toward the second floor. While he was limping, he was also reaching down his pants. I chased him up the stairs and saw that he was hiding behind the bedroom door. I slammed the door open, reached behind, and grabbed him, pushing him facedown on the floor. I then handcuffed him, searched him, and found he was wearing two pairs of pants, each a different color. I also found on the inside pair of pants a pistol in his pocket. That's when I realized what he was reaching for when he was going up the stairs and put his hand in his pants. One of my rounds had shot him in his right leg—the same side where the weapon was hidden.

Uniformed officers arrived shortly after that, and the defendant was taken to Hahnemann University Hospital. I went to Philadelphia General Hospital, where I was treated for my head wound. After leaving the hospital, I was taken to the police administration building because I had fired my weapon. As we were going inside, Police Commissioner O'Neill was coming out. The detective in charge of the case told the commissioner that I was the officer who made the arrest. The COMMISSIONER looked at me and told me to get a haircut. I was then detailed to the homicide division while the investigation of the incident was ongoing, which was normal procedure whenever an officer fired his or her weapon. I asked them what I would be doing while in the homicide division, and they told me I would be sitting at a desk. I could go out for lunch or take a walk, but I could not get involved in anything. This went on for three days. I called my captain—Captain Ansel—and asked if he could do anything. He made some calls, and I was then sent down to work in the photo lab. To my surprise, the officer in charge of the photo lab was Jim Kelly, the same officer from when I worked with Joe Charles, the same guy who would stop and check on my best friend Jerry Farmer when we worked on cars with Joe Charles. He was also the same guy who said I should join the police department when I returned from Vietnam.

After about a month, I was back working in the burglary detail. The man I apprehended was positively identified as the male who was holding up various doctors' offices and other establishments in the area.

March 15, 1973

Officer Forjohn and I were working the Eighteenth District Rape Detail due to the number of rapes occurring around the University of Pennsylvania when we observed two males at Fortieth and Chestnut Streets running away from a parked car with the hood raised up. A male was inside the car, yelling for help. We gave chase and apprehended them. After we checked them for weapons, we cuffed them and returned them to the parked car, where the occupant in the car identified them as the ones who had robbed him at knifepoint. The two suspects were taken to west detectives.

December 27, 1973

While riding around in our car, Officer Forjohn and I noticed two males acting in a suspicious manner in the area of Twenty-first and Waverly Streets. We put them under surveillance, and after a short time observing them, they attempted to rob a man at knifepoint. We gave pursuit, and after a short chase, we arrested both of them.

February 27, 1974

While driving alone in the area of Broad and Lombard Streets around 7:00 p.m., I observed a uniformed officer pursuing a male. I jumped from my car and apprehended the male. The officer who was chasing the subject was Officer Hebbons of the Seventeenth District. The suspect was wanted for a robbery that had occurred minutes before at 1714 Pine Street. The Seventeenth District bordered my district, the Ninth.

March 12, 1974

As we drove around our district on this day, we were a four-man team because 9BD2 was riding with us. When in the area of Juniper and Arch Streets, we saw an elderly man being robbed by four males. We chased and apprehended the males. We called for a patrol wagon, which picked them up and took them back to the scene of the crime, where they were positively identified by the elderly complainant.

March 16, 1974

Riding around the lower end of the district around 8:00 p.m., Officer Forjohn and I observed two juvenile males looking around and acting suspiciously. We decided to keep a watch on them. We followed them for a few blocks. When at Sixteenth and Lombard Streets, they tried to rob a man who was walking down the street. We then arrested both young men at the scene.

May 22, 1974

Working as a three-man team with my partner Officer Forjohn and Officer Pisco, from 9BD2 and driving in the area of Nineteenth and Market Streets around 7:00 p.m., we observed one of two males with a shotgun hidden underneath his coat. We walked separately by the male, and when we were close enough, we arrested him. We found the shotgun to be fully loaded. Subsequent investigation disclosed that the male and his accomplice were involved in a series of armed robberies.

August 15, 1974

While working the burglary detail with Officer Clements from 9BD2, we responded to a radio call of a strong-arm robbery in the Sixth District at Eleventh and Market Streets. Being only a few blocks away, we radioed that we were going in. We were the Ninth District BD, but the Sixth District was just three blocks away.

When coming into the area, we received flash information over the police radio, giving us a description of the wanted men. At Eleventh and Locust Streets in the Sixth District, we spotted two males fitting the description. We apprehended both males, who were returned by police wagon to the crime scene, where they were both positively identified by the complainant.

October 23, 1975

As we were patrolling the upper end of the Ninth District (the Fairmount section), we responded to a radio call of a robbery at Twentieth and Wallace Streets. At the time the call came in, we were in that area, and at Nineteenth and Mt. Vernon Streets, we spotted three males who fit the description of the suspects put out on police radio. We then pursued and caught all three males. We called for a patrol wagon, and the males were taken back to Twentieth and Wallace Streets, where the crime took place. All three males were positively identified by the victim and arrested.

April 22, 1977

While patrolling the lower end of the Ninth District around 4:30 p.m., we started watching a male in the area of Twentieth and Lombard Streets. After just a few minutes, we lost sight of him, but we stayed in the area. About ten minutes passed, and while driving around 1900 Lombard Street, we heard a yell. We then saw the male we had been observing running down the street. We quickly apprehended him and took him back to the area of 1900 Lombard Street, where he was positively identified by the complainants who said the man had just robbed them.

October 30, 1978

While leaving district headquarters at Twentieth and Callowhill Streets, driving north on Twentieth, Pete and I observed a car with three males inside pull over, get out of their car, and forcibly abduct an elderly man who was walking north on Twentieth Street. They then drove north on Twentieth Street, crossed over Poplar Street, into the Twenty-third District. They turned onto a side street and stopped the car.

I got out of Pete's car, and then Pete drove around the corner to block the other end of the small street. I saw the males pull the elderly man from the vehicle, knock him to the ground, and start going through his pockets. I radioed Pete to call for backup. I then started toward the males. I identified myself as police, and the males took off running, leaving the vehicle behind. After a lengthy pursuit, we apprehended two of the three males.

Less than a month later, a report came over the police radio of several males stealing a motorcycle. The description fit one of the males we arrested from the kidnapping charges. Because we had his address from police records, Pete Forjohn, John Pisco, Frank Dembeck from 9BD2, and I took up surveillance of the defendant's address. Not long after did one of the two males previously arrested pull up on the stolen motorcycle. We then called for a wagon and placed him under arrest. All he could be charged with, however, was receiving stolen property.

December 16, 1978, to January 12, 1979

The 9BD1 and 9BD2 were involved in the investigations of twenty-two robberies of elderly persons in their residences in the Spring Garden section of the Ninth District. These residents were being robbed of their Social Security money, among other things.

Officer Forjohn, Officer Dembeck, Officer Pisco, and I started patrolling the area around the times elderly residents received their Social Security checks. We would split up and hang around banks where the elderly would cash their checks. Also, because we noticed that most elderly persons would be walking to and from the banks on Spring Garden Street, we started driving somewhat behind them as they walked home. While driving, we noticed a car slow down in front of a home of a person who just cashed his check. We then passed the car as it pulled over in front of the house. We recognized the males inside the car as the same ones who had been arrested in October 3, 1978, for robbery and kidnapping—then later for stealing a motorcycle. We did not stop the males, for we had no proof they were committing the robberies, but in our minds, we knew. We took down the address of the home and hung out for several hours after our tour of duty was over. The next morning, we read the part 1 crime sheet and found a report that the house we had been watching was robbed by a group of males during the night. We gave the information we had gathered from the night before, along with photos of the males, because we had arrested them several times before.

Central detectives took a group of photos to the residence of the robbery, and the males who robbed them were picked out of a group of photos they were shown. The males were then arrested. The eight defendants were then charged with twenty-nine robberies and burglaries.

Chapter 8

THEFT FROM VEHICLES AND BURGLARY OF VEHICLES

Theft from auto is when someone walks by vehicles and tries car doors to see if any are unlocked. If that person finds one that is unlocked, they then enter the vehicle and take whatever items they want from the vehicle (a lesser charge by police).

A burglary of a vehicle is when someone breaks into a car using a tool such as a screwdriver or a coat hanger or by breaking a window. The burglary of a vehicle is a part 1 offense, and charges are then applied.

There were many burglaries of vehicle arrests made by 9BD1. We learned it was easy to spot someone who was going to burglarize an automobile. A normal person walking down the sidewalk walks in the middle of the sidewalk, but someone looking to break into a car walks close to the street side of the walk. They look into every car they pass until they find one that has items in it, such as briefcases, packages, or other things of value.

We noticed that once someone saw things of value in a car, they would stand on the sidewalk, look around to see if anyone was in the area, and if not, would use tools—most often a coat hanger and a screwdriver—to open the vehicle. The screwdriver would be used to make an opening between the car door or window that would allow for the insertion of a coat hanger, which would go through the window and lift the lock button on the car. They would then enter the car and take the items inside. The 9BD1 would then approach and make the arrest.

After the arrest, the thief was taken to CDD by a patrol wagon. The items taken from the vehicle were transported to CDD by 9BD2. The 9BD1 also left a message inside the vehicle, instructing the car's owner to contact CDD to retrieve their possessions and press charges.

Several times, 9BD2 would follow a male who was looking into autos for a long time before the suspect(s) found a vehicle they wanted to get into. One such time, 9BD1 observed a male looking into autos and so set up a surveillance of him. After a period of time watching him and the male being very cautious (always looking around), we decided it was best not to follow him in our vehicle. So I went on foot, following the male from about a block away, while Pete followed in the private vehicle—keeping one block or so from the area. After an hour of following the male, I radioed Pete to pick me up so we could switch places, for the male looking into the autos was very cautious of anyone following him and perhaps had spotted me. We traded places, and Pete took up the foot surveillance. After another half hour or so, the male entered a large parking lot. It had also started getting dark, which made it more difficult to follow him.

The man was looking into all the cars in the parking lot. Pete thought the male had spotted him, so he started looking into the parked cars as well. The male saw Pete looking into the cars and approached him. It seemed he thought that Pete wanted to break into an auto also. The male then stated that he had found an auto he wanted to break into and asked Pete if he would be a lookout for him. He added that he would do the same for him, and Pete said he had already found a car he wanted to break into, so the agreement was made.

As soon as the male broke into the car, I showed up in our vehicle, and Pete and I made the arrest. The defendant couldn't believe we were cops! This man had a long, extensive record for burglary of autos. He told us he "never felt so stupid."

Another time while following a male looking into autos, I was on foot following him while Pete was patrolling in his car. I followed the male into a very large parking lot with several different levels. It was very difficult to tail this man because of the levels of the lot, with the male constantly changing direction while walking through the lot.

It looked like he found a car he was interested in and then walked away. I started to follow when the male turned and started back in my direction. I crawled under a vehicle to hide and shut off my walkie-talkie. The male then started to break into the very car I was hiding under! He gained entry to the vehicle, took several items, and then started to leave the parking lot. When he was far enough away from the vehicle he had broken into, I called Pete on the walkie-talkie and informed him what just happened. Pete exited his vehicle and waited for the man to leave the parking lot at the same time I was following behind the man. As the man was about to leave the parking lot, we converged on him and made the arrest.

The defendant told both of us he had found the items lying beside the vehicle. I told him I happened to be under the vehicle he had broken into. Needless to say, when the trial came up, he pleaded guilty to the burglary of an auto.

Christmas

There were always burglaries of autos during the Christmas season, and 9BD1 made many arrests, but one arrest opened some eyes, so to speak. We were following a male suspect who was looking into cars as he passed them in the 2000 block of Sansom Street. It was a few days before Christmas, and night had fallen. Sansom Street was crowded with people shopping for last-minute Christmas gifts. We observed the male stop by a car, looking all around. When the foot traffic slowed down around him, he broke into a red car and took several wrapped Christmas gifts.

As the male walked east on Sansom Street, I exited our vehicle while Pete tried to drive through traffic to get to the end of Sansom Street to block off the male. I approached the man and identified myself as police. The male then threw the packages at me and ran east on Sansom Street. I tackled him on the sidewalk, and a scuffle ensued.

Just as I was placing handcuffs on the male, a White woman started yelling at me to "leave that poor Black guy alone." I advised the woman that I was the police, but she continued to yell at me.

Shortly after the arrest, Pete arrived, and the defendant was under control. We then called for a patrol wagon to transport the thief. As Pete had control of the defendant and the Christmas gifts, I went back to the car that had been burglarized or broken into in order to leave a message in the car for the owner to contact CDD.

Lo and behold, the car, along with all the Christmas gifts, belonged to the White woman who was yelling at me while I was arresting the Black guy who had stolen from her. She was very thankful to both Pete and me after that.

As always, people complain about the actions taken by police, not knowing the circumstances of the arrest.

Special Recognition

One night, we observed a male breaking into a car and taking a tape deck from the vehicle. As we attempted to arrest the male, he started running east on Ranstead Street, where, after I caught up with him, I tackled and handcuffed him. It was then that the police commissioner, Frank Rizzo, came through the rear door of a nearby building. We were outside Frank Rizzo's campaign headquarters— for he happened to be running for mayor of Philadelphia at the time.

He asked what the problem was, and we told him we were the Ninth District Burglary Detail and the reason we had just made the arrest. He told us, "Great job!" then said, "I've heard nothing but good work being done by 9BD." Commissioner Rizzo also said that we were well known at the police headquarters administration building.

The Arrest that Really Stood Out

Of the many auto burglary arrests we made in thirteen years, there was one that really stood out.

While driving north on Eighteenth Street around Walnut Street, we observed a well-dressed, sharp-looking male with gray hair wearing a tuxedo standing along the wall of a building. We guessed he was around fifty years old. Pete and I passed him in our car and stopped at a red light. Pete, who was driving, looked in the rearview mirror and observed the well-dressed man walk up to the parked car on Eighteenth Street, look inside the vehicle, then back away when a pedestrian walked by.

We looked at each other and said, "You've got to be kidding!" We drove around the block, and Pete dropped me off at Walnut and Eighteenth Streets and drove to Eighteenth and Sansom Streets and parked his car. We then took up a surveillance of the male.

We saw that the man stood against the wall until there was no foot traffic then walked up to a car. He then placed a wire coat hanger through the passenger side of the vehicle and, after a very short time, popped the lock. He entered the car, took a brown leather briefcase from the back seat, and started walking south on Eighteenth Street straight toward me.

As he approached Walnut Street, I identified myself and told him he was under arrest for burglary of the auto. Without being told to, he put his hands in the air and placed them on the wall of a building so we could pat him down for weapons. The man was very polite, spoke like an educated man, and had a really neat name— Amos Otis—along with a lengthy record of arrests. We placed him in Pete's car and took him to CDD along with the briefcase.

After about an hour, the owner of the burglarized car came into CDD. He was a lawyer for the electrical union, and the briefcase contained the original new contract for the union. Needless to say, the lawyer was very thankful and offered both Pete and me $20— which we both refused. Instead, we asked him to send a nice letter to the police commissioner, which he did.

Less than a month after the arrest of Amos Otis, Pete and I spotted him again—still in his tuxedo—this time on Sixteenth Street. We both watched him break into another car then started walking north. Pete and I were south of him. I yelled to Amos to stop and place his hands on the nearest wall. To our amazement, Amos did just that. We placed him under arrest once again.

After that, we never ran into Amos again.

Chapter 9

RESPONDING TO SUICIDE ATTEMPTS AND OTHER CALLS FOR HELP

Suicide Attempts

Pete and I, along with uniformed Police Officer Tony Miller, responded to a possible suicide at the Drake Hotel, located at Seventeenth and Spruce Streets, one evening around 8:00 p.m. After a search of the area without finding anyone, we decided to go to the roof of the hotel. Once up there, we happened to look down at the lower roof and noticed a man's head sticking out.

Then we heard him moaning. We called the police radio, who then notified the fire department to check it out. It turns out the man had jumped from the upper roof to the lower roof and fell through the lower roof up to his head. The fire department rescued him and took him to Hannamen Hospital.

While working the 2:00 p.m. to 10:00 p.m. shift, Pete and I responded to a possible suicide attempt around Twenty-third and Delancy Streets. We heard the radio call come over the police radio, and we were in the area, so we went in. When we arrived, there were several uniformed officers on the scene.

There was a woman about thirty years old standing on the third-floor balcony. She kept saying she couldn't take it anymore and wanted it to be over. I, along with the uniformed officer, started talking to her. After a few minutes, the woman said I could come up to her apartment to talk—through the door.

We spoke for fifteen minutes or so, and eventually, she let me in. She told me she was a psychologist and that she couldn't handle it anymore. I told her how important she was to her clients and how much help she was to them. After a while, she agreed to come downstairs to ask for help for herself.

About a month later, Pete and I were called to appear at a hearing before other doctors at the Women's Medical College, located on Henry Avenue in Philadelphia. It was a hearing for the female psychologist before the medical board. I testified to the incident, and we left. We found out later that the woman was allowed to keep practicing.

About four months later, the call came over the police radio about a possible suicide attempt. Lo and behold—it was the same woman! Again, we responded and talked her out of suicide. We were never notified of another hearing for her and never saw or heard about her again.

A Most Bizarre Story

Among the arrests we made for burglary, there was this one couple who stands out in my memory.

As we were patrolling the lower end of the district, around Twenty-second Street, we noticed two White males talking by the rear of a vehicle. Standing at the door of a nearby apartment was a white, blond-haired female who was looking up and down Twenty-second Street. Pete and I pulled over around the corner and took up surveillance. Something just didn't seem right to us.

After a short time, we observed one male opened the trunk of his car and pulled out two rifles. Both men then entered the apartment where the blond woman was standing. We waited until the guy who had taken the rifles from the trunk of his car left the apartment without the rifles and drove away. We then followed him a short distance before calling the police radio to have a patrol car pull him over.

Once he was pulled over, we identified ourselves as police and told him what we observed him do and then asked him about the rifles. He told us he had a drug problem, that the rifles were his, and that he traded them for drugs. The man was then taken to central detectives.

We then got the names of the two people who lived in the apartment from the male taken into custody, and a warrant was made out for them. Along with uniformed officers, Pete and I served the warrant and confiscated the rifles along with a small amount of narcotic drugs. Both the male and the female were taken to central detectives for booking.

They were both released on bail along with the guy who swapped his rifles for narcotics. We came in contact with the male and female several times after that on the street. They were boyfriend and girlfriend, living together with a drug problem, but were not thieves or violent. They both had a drug problem and were seriously trying to get help.

Six months passed since their arrest, and Pete and I hadn't seen them for a while. It was summer. A call came over the police radio about a female on top of a sixty-foot crane on a floating barge in the Schuylkill River! She held police and fire rescuers at bay by inching further up the crane when they were trying to get her to come down.

While police said the twenty-six-year-old woman, who was bloodied from superficial wounds, never actually threatened to jump to her death, she did remove her blouse.

Pete and I responded to the radio call. When we arrived, we saw that it was Wendy Lombardi, the same woman we had arrested along with her boyfriend. The police lieutenant, who was on the scene, didn't like Pete and me for some reason and ordered us to leave. We never knew why he didn't like us since we hardly had any contact with him while we were on the job. But we followed his orders and left the scene.

After about ten minutes went by, the police radio called for us to return to the area and report to the lieutenant. When we arrived, the lieutenant told me that the young woman would only come down if I went up to get her. I went over to the crane where the Philadelphia Fire Department hooked me up in a safety harness. I then climbed the crane, talked to Wendy, and with the assistance of the fireman, brought her safely down the crane, where she was then placed in the patrol wagon and taken to the hospital for observation.

Nothing further was ever said to Pete and me by the lieutenant. When we got into our car, I said to Pete, "Boy, he must really dislike us now!"

The next morning, Pete and I went to the captain's office to pick up our walkie-talkies when the civilian clerk, Laura, said to us, "Good job!" I asked her what she was talking about, and she showed me the front page of the newspaper. There on the front page was a picture of me, along with the fireman, bringing Wendy down from the crane. Pete looked at me and said, "The Lieutenant's dislike for us just became pure hatred!" Little did we know, he would get even several years later.

Chapter 10

$$\sim\!\!\approx\!\!\sim$$

THE STORY OF AN ATTEMPTED RAPE AND THE EVENTS THAT FOLLOWED

Late one summer evening, Pete and I were riding in the area of Nineteenth and Pine Streets when we observed a male trying to open apartment doors. I exited our vehicle and took up a surveillance of the man while Pete continued to ride around the block in our car.

I positioned myself in a small alcove behind a tree, where I could track the man's movements. I saw him break into the front vestibule door of an apartment building and radioed Pete to describe what I had observed. Pete joined me, and we both went into the building, which we saw was divided into four apartments. We didn't know which apartment the man had entered, so we went to each apartment door to listen, hoping to overhear something. When we reached the third door, we heard a female voice begging someone not to hurt her.

The door was locked, so we decided to kick it in. We discovered the male attempting to rape the female. A short scuffle ensued before the male was handcuffed and placed under arrest. Found in his possession were a screwdriver and a knife. We called for a patrol wagon to take the prisoner to central detectives for processing, and we took the female to central detectives so she could give a statement about the attack then be transferred to the sex crimes unit. The male was charged with attempted rape, burglary, and other charges.

On the day of the trial, a very cold day in November, the courtroom was full of students on a field trip from a school in South Philadelphia. The defendant had a public defender as his attorney, whose name was Merryweather. As I finished giving my testimony, the court recessed for lunch.

After lunch, Merryweather called me back to the stand. He said, "Officer Porter, in your testimony, you said you positioned yourself in an alcove across the street where my defendant could not see you because of a bush that hid you from sight."

I answered, "That is correct."

The defense attorney then said he went to the small alcove where I said I took up the surveillance. He said he also stood across the street from the apartment his client broke into. From that standpoint, he could clearly see the alcove where I said I had been hiding, and if he could see it, then the defendant could have seen it too since I had said the man was continually looking around. He then asked me if I would like to rephrase my statement. I told him, "No, I would not."

I then stated to him and the court that the surveillance was in the summer and that the bush at that time was covered with leaves, whereas now, in November, there were no leaves on the bush. Also, my surveillance was in the evening, not during daylight.

The defendant was found guilty and sent to prison. A week or so later, I was called into the captain's office. He told me that the school class present at the trial enjoyed it so much that the school's principal wanted me to appear and talk to the students about the police department and how trials are conducted.

I wasn't thrilled about going to the school to talk to the students, but I accepted the invitation. I had never spoken to a group of students or a class before. Nevertheless, as apprehensive as I was, I went to the school, which was located on Susquehanna Avenue.

I was met by the principal, who told me I was scheduled to speak to two different classes in the morning and one class after lunch. In the first class, there were a few students who had been present at the trial. They asked me some very good questions about the court system and police work. By the time I got to the second class, I felt a little more comfortable talking to the students.

We then broke for lunch, and I was invited to join a male teacher from the second class. When we entered the teacher's cafeteria, the man introduced me to the other teachers, who basically ignored me. In fact, the teacher who escorted me to the cafeteria and I were the lone occupants of our table. The teacher apologized for the rudeness of the other teachers, but I told him it was okay and to be expected.

Several weeks later, the captain called me into his office and handed me a bunch of letters from the students I had spoken to. There were close to fifty letters thanking me for talking with them. That made the whole thing worth it!

At the time, I was living at an apartment complex called Summit Park East. Most of those who lived there were single, and many were schoolteachers. Those who I got to know would tell me I only see the bad things in life. I would tell them I see the good and the bad in everyday life and that they had spent their whole lives in school then college then the classroom, not knowing too much about society itself. Some understood where I was coming from, and we got along just fine. They also liked having me living at the complex, especially after I made several arrests there for burglary of the residents' apartments while I was living there!

Later that summer, Pete and I were driving in the area of Twenty-second and Arch Streets, where we observed a minor automobile accident. One car was a convertible with the top down, driven by a male wearing a "super-fly" hat (wide-rimmed fedora), which was the style then. As we approached the scene, we realized that the male was the public defender, Merryweather, at the previous rape trial. We got out of our car and identified ourselves, and he immediately recognized us.

Pete and I got together and decided to have some fun with the public defender. He started to tell us about the accident, which we already knew was minor, but we told him to wait until we talked to the other party involved. As Pete was talking to the other driver, I walked over to the public defender and told him that Pete and I had observed the whole thing. I then asked him for his drivers' license and registration card. I told him that it was his fault and that he'd better call his insurance company. He asked me to give him a break and that he was running in the next election for a judgeship.

I told him to sit in his automobile while I called for a uniformed officer to write up an accident report. During this time, Pete was talking to the other driver, who stated that they just bumped into each other and that there were no damages or injuries.

We could see that the public defender was a nervous wreck. When the uniformed officer showed up, Pete and I spoke with him, explained what happened and that we were playing a little joke on the public defender.

We knew there were no damages, and the other party didn't wish to report the minor accident. Pete and I talked to the public defender, who again asked for a break. We told him we would talk to the uniformed officer (who was then in on the joke) on his behalf. The uniformed officer then told Merryweather that Pete and I had asked him to give him a break, so he was only going to write up an incident report—minor disturbance (unfounded)—which meant police were not needed. Both parties to the accident were satisfied. Merryweather could not thank us enough. He asked if we could vote for him in the next election, which we did.

The only time we saw him again was in the Ninth Police District. Pete and I were reporting to work on the 10:00 a.m. to 6:00 p.m. shift. As we walked into the building, we passed through the hearing room where Judge Merryweather was presiding. We noticed that the judge had a bad case of hiccups. We then approached the court coordinator, a uniformed officer who we knew as Tony Melchiorre. We asked him if anyone had tried to help the judge with the hiccups. He told us they had tried everything with no success.

I asked Officer Melchiorre if I could talk to the judge. He approached the judge, said something to him, and pointed to Pete and me. Judge Merryweather called for a short recess and stepped down from the bench. He approached Pete and me, said hello and that it was nice to see us. I told him I could get rid of those hiccups for him.

We went into a side office, and I got the judge a large glass of water then handed him a pencil. I told him to put the pencil in his mouth horizontally and, with the pencil in his mouth, drink down the glass of water, which he did. His hiccups stopped immediately.

All he said to Pete and me was "You guys are something else." Then he went back to the courtroom and continued the hearings. During the remainder of our time in the police department, we never ran into Judge Merryweather again.

Years later, we heard of the judge's passing, only to find out that he was in Vietnam at the same time as I was and that he was in the same areas I was in, but we had never come into contact with each other. He was also a decorated soldier.

He's one of the few people I think about often and wish I had known him better. He had a great record as a judge and was well-liked.

Chapter 11

RAPE

While covering the 2000 block of Walnut Street, Pete and I saw a young female, along with an older male, causing a disturbance on the sidewalk. The older male grabbed the young female and started to pull her down the street.

We got out of our unmarked car and approached the male and female. We identified ourselves as police, at which time the female yelled out that the male had raped her. The male then tried to flee but was very quickly apprehended and arrested. It turned out that the young female was a runaway. She had been befriended by the older male, who then took her to his apartment, where he forcibly kept her for several days and forcibly raped her several times.

The young girl finally managed to get out of the apartment, only to be pursued by the older male. This is when we came upon them and apprehended him. The male was charged with statutory rape, corrupting a minor, and harboring a runaway.

July and August 1975

During the months of July and August, a number of robberies and sexual assaults on women were occurring in the area of the 2300 block of JFK Boulevard. They happened as women were crossing the JFK Bridge toward Thirtieth and Market Streets. The male would grab them and pull them into a field next to the boulevard.

My partner Officer Forjohn and I decided to patrol that area only. I was driving, and Pete was the passenger in our unmarked vehicle. After an hour or so, I had Pete drive into the police district with my vehicle so we could switch cars. We did that. So if the perpetrator was in the area, he would not see the same car going up and down the boulevard.

Shortly after Pete returned in his car, we spotted the suspect in the field. I had Pete drop me off, and I walked down the side street and positioned myself so I could observe the male. I saw him walk toward females as they crossed the bridge, but he made no attempt to rob or assault them. After about thirty minutes, I told Pete I was going to apprehend the male and for him to come in. As I tried to get closer to the man, he took off north through the field. I gave pursuit and caught up with him at the end of the field where there was a wall. On the other side of the wall was a thirty-foot drop to the train tracks.

The male put up a fight, and as I was in the process of securing him, Pete came over and, for some reason, thought I was going to drop the man over the wall. In fact, I had him leaning over the wall to place handcuffs on him. Pete said, "Don't do it!" and I assumed he meant don't drop him over the wall.

The suspect must have thought I was going to drop him over as well since he said, "I'm sorry, please don't do it."

The suspect was taken to the central detective division. After a lineup, he was positively identified for the robberies and the rape. At the trial, one woman who was assaulted and robbed was from England, and she returned to testify against him. The male was charged with rape, robbery, and assault, as well as other miscellaneous charges.

Chapter 12

FENCES

A fence is someone who buys stolen property at a cheap price, only to resell it for a profit.

During these times, there were a lot of junkies who would steal or burglarize a home, take the items to a fence that they knew, and try to sell them the stolen items—usually getting only a fraction of what the items were worth—maybe a little more if it were jewelry, just so they could buy drugs.

There were these two people who lived next door to Town Pizza at Nineteenth and Pine Streets, the very place where Pete and I ate lunch every day. We were informed that these two people did not work and that there were always young people going in and out of the apartments, only staying a short time. After learning this, Pete and I set up a surveillance of these apartments.

One day, the male and female came out of the apartment and got into their car, so we followed them. They drove to a South Philadelphia jewelry shop. Pete got out of our vehicle and entered the shop, where he observed the male and female selling jewelry and silverware to the jeweler.

We then decided we should again set up a surveillance of their apartment because we would need more information if we wanted to get a search warrant for the apartment. We set up a periodic surveillance on them when we able to. One day, we observed a male carrying what appeared to be a heavy item wrapped in a green trash bag, walking to the apartment. He went into the apartment, only to leave a short time later without the green trash bag. He got into his car, and we followed him. We ran the license tag on his car through police radio, only to learn it was a stolen vehicle. We then asked the police radio to have the car stopped. It was pulled over a few blocks later, and the male was arrested.

We called for a patrol wagon to take the male to central detectives. Pete drove the stolen car to the Ninth District. While the male was being processed at central detectives, we asked him about the green trash bag and its contents. He told us the man who lived in the apartment bought the stolen items from him. It was a record player and components that he had stolen from a home in West Philadelphia. He also told us he had stolen items before. This gave us enough information to obtain a search warrant for the apartment.

Later that day, with our search warrant in hand, along with two detectives from central detectives, we hit the apartment. To our surprise, we didn't find anything more than the record player at first. But after a while and the discovery and search of a false ceiling, we found a black case containing monogrammed silverware that had been reported stolen.

The male defendant got really cocky, telling us we were about a week late. We assumed this meant he had gotten rid of a lot of stuff. Both the man and the woman were taken to CDD, where they gave false identifications. They were then sent down to the roundhouse (police headquarters), where they were fingerprinted, which revealed their true identities. Both were wanted for forgery, theft, receiving stolen property, and other miscellaneous charges. They made bail, and a week later, both moved out of their apartment.

We didn't have to go to trial for the case because they both pleaded guilty to the offenses. We never found out how much time they got, but we were informed they were sent out of state.

Jewelry Store Fence—Burglary, Receiving Stolen Property

While most jewelry shops in Philadelphia were very honest, there were several that had no problem buying stolen jewelry. There was one incident where 9BD1 and 9BD2 worked together to make an arrest of four males, ages fourteen to sixteen, who we observed enter a jewelry shop in the 1900 block of Chestnut Street. We saw them enter the shop, leave a short time later, and then return a short time after that.

I went into the shop, pretending to be interested in buying a watch. I observed the young males hand several pieces of jewelry to a middle-aged woman behind another counter in the store. I walked out of the shop and told Pete and two other officers from 9BD1 and 9BD2 about what I had just observed. Together, we decided that I would go back into the shop while they would call the shop and tell whoever answered the phone that the young males were being watched by police.

As I entered the shop, still under the guise of looking at watches, I heard the woman behind the counter tell the four juveniles that she could give them $300 for all the items. The woman then told one of her employees, who we later learned was a Russian illegal, to take the jewelry items downstairs and melt them.

The phone then rang in the shop, and the woman answered it. She quickly hung up and told the four juveniles to get out of the store and that the cops were watching them. Then she yelled down the stairs to the guy she had given the jewelry to, telling him to hide the items. At that time, I identified myself as police, and the four juveniles ran out of the shop, only to be apprehended by the BD teams. I then ran down the stairs, where I caught the male melting a piece of jewelry while trying to hide the other pieces. Upstairs, my partner Pete entered the shop and took the female into custody. There were two other employees in the showroom of the shop who was told to stay in place, which they did.

We called a patrol wagon to transport all those involved at the jewelry shop to central detectives and another patrol wagon to transport the juvenile defendants to the juvenile ADE division.

Further investigation found that the jewelry had been taken from a home during a burglary earlier that day, and it was not the first time these juveniles had done business with the jewelry shop. The owners were arrested and charged with receiving stolen property, as well as being a fencing operation. Sadly, about a year later, these same people reopened the jewelry shop.

Chapter 13

$\sim$

THEFTS IN OFFICE BUILDINGS AND BUSINESSES

There had been reports of women and some men having their purses or wallets stolen while working in office buildings in the Ninth District. It was hard to catch this type of thief due to the many office buildings in the area.

One day, while Pete and I were working the 2:00 p.m. to 10:00 p.m. tour of duty, we were asked by our captain to interview some female employees at a women's clothing store. This store had been robbed the night before by four Black men armed with shotguns and a rifle. We went to the shop and talked to a woman who gave us a description of the males.

Being that we were up against males with shotguns, I decided to carry a backup pistol under my coat. Instead of just a snub-nosed 38 caliber pistol, I carried a 44-magnum pistol for backup, which was not legal according to police regulations, but I wasn't taking any chances in the event we came in contact with the holdup men.

That same evening around 7:00 p.m., while traveling in the area of 1800 Delancey Street, we observed three males who somewhat fit the description (height and clothing) given by the female at the clothing shop. They were standing at the bottom steps of a home—then walked east on Delancey Street, only to return to the same house. Then the tallest of the three males walked up the steps and knocked on the door.

A middle-aged White female answered the door and had what appeared to be a short conversation with the man. He then left, and the three males walked east on Delancey Street again.

Pete kept an eye on the males from his auto, and I walked up to the home, rang the bell, and identified myself as police when the woman answered. I asked her about the male. She told me her purse had been stolen earlier that day and that the male offered to return it to her for a $50 reward. He told her he found it on the street with her ID, but there was no money in it. The woman told him she had already reported the contents stolen, that the credit cards and other items were going to be replaced.

I called Pete on the radio, and he told me the three men had walked south on Eighteenth Street, where the tallest of the three entered a black bar called The Brown Bomber at Eighteenth and South Street. I quickly ran to that location. When I arrived, Pete called for a uniformed patrol car to meet us there.

When uniformed officers arrived, we placed the two males under arrest, and they were put in a patrol wagon. They were informed that they were being taken to CDD for investigation of a robbery. The third male was still inside The Brown Bomber. I walked into the bar to see if I could locate him. As soon as I walked into the bar, everyone stopped talking and looked at me as if to say, "What are you doing here?" I immediately identified myself as police and then saw the male I was looking for at the very end of the bar.

I asked the man if he would step outside—at which time several bar patrons told him he didn't have to do anything. They also told me to leave. Thinking I had backup behind me, meaning uniformed police, and fearing a major confrontation, I pulled out my 44-magnum from under my coat and again asked the male to step outside. This time, the other men in the bar, who had told him not to go, said, "You better go with the cop."

When he walked up to me and we turned to leave the bar, I realized there was no one there to back me up. Uniform patrol had left with the two other males, and Pete was holding yet another male outside.

After the males were taken to the CDD division, it was decided that these were not the males who committed the holdup of the clothing store. They were charged, however, with receiving stolen property—the woman's pocketbook from Delancey Street. They said they paid some boys $10 for the stolen pocketbook in the hopes of making money for returning it to the victim. All the males had prior arrest records for theft.

Not one week later, Pete and I were patrolling in the area of Nineteenth and Spruce Street where we observed the tall Black man we had just arrested at the Brown Bomber bar came out of an office building, walked around the corner, and started going through a woman's wallet. We placed him under arrest for theft. He told us he found it on the street. We took him, who we called Harold B., to CDD, where he was charged with theft and receiving stolen property.

A few days later, we once again observed him coming out of another office building. This time, he jumped on a bus. I was driving, so I drove to the next bus stop, where my partner Pete got on the bus. Pete walked to the back of the bus, where he observed Harold B. pull out a lady's purse from his coat pocket and start rifling through it. Pete informed me via radio what he had observed. I then got in front of the bus and stopped it. I entered the bus and walked to the rear, where Pete and I placed the male under arrest again. We took him, once again, to CDD for processing. While en route, the man asked us why he kept getting caught by us. We told him that the first time we arrested him, he was put in a cell at central detectives, and he fell asleep. While he was asleep, we put a tracking device in his ear, so we knew everywhere he went. We told him we would take it out if he stopped stealing in the Ninth District and if he would promise not to come west of Broad Street again.

He promised he wouldn't, so we told him that we deactivated the sensor. We then told the Sixth District Burglary Detail—who covered the east side of Broad Street—to be on the lookout for him. Pete and I never came in contact with him again.

Chapter 14

THEFT OF AUTOMOBILE

Just a few of the many thefts of automobile arrests…one of the easier ones—Pete and I were covering the area of Broad Street when I was driving. We stopped at a red light, and a car pulled up next to us. As I looked over at the car, I could see that the ignition on the Chevy steering column had a rag covering it.

As the light turned green, Pete called in the tag number, along with a description of the car. Police radioed to us that the car had been reported stolen that very morning. We then called for a uniformed Ninth District patrol car to assist us in stopping the auto. As we were on our own unmarked cars and in plain clothes, it was always prudent to call in uniformed officers for assistance. The auto was stopped by uniformed patrol, as well as by Pete and me, and the male was arrested for auto theft.

Another instance occurred one night when Pete and I were in the area of Eighteenth and Spring Garden Streets, and we observed a couple of males acting in a suspicious manner. I got out of the car, and Pete drove it around the corner.

The males I was watching dispersed and went their own ways. In the meantime, Pete radioed me that he was observing four other Puerto Rican males in a parking lot around the corner. As I started walking south on Eighteenth Street, Pete radioed me that they just broke into a car and stole it. They were headed in my direction on

Eighteenth Street. I was on foot when I saw the car coming toward me.

Pete radioed me that he was trying to get to me, but he was stuck in traffic behind a truck. I stood in the middle of the street, pulled out my police badge, and yelled, "Stop!" I had never expected the car to stop, but it did. I then said the only command I knew in Spanish, "Laventa las manos," hoping it meant, "Put your hands in the air," which they did. Pete arrived, and we placed the four males under arrest. After that, they were taken by uniform patrol wagon to the Ninth District and turned over to the juvenile aid division.

Another time, Pete and I set up surveillance at a large apartment complex located at 2401 Pennsylvania Avenue because there had been reports of autos being stolen from their parking lot. That day, I had borrowed my good friend Jerry Farmer's car, a Volkswagen. Jerry was repairing my car because I had driven it down the art museum steps in pursuit of a purse snatcher. We caught the perpetrator, but there was severe damage to my car.

Pete went onto the roof of the 2401 apartment building with a pair of binoculars. I remained in the parking lot area parked in the Volkswagen. After about an hour and a half, Pete radioed me that he spotted two males breaking into a red Plymouth Fury. I radioed back to Pete to head down to assist in the arrest. I then observed two Puerto Rican males enter the vehicle. When I approached the auto, I saw one male working on the ignition. I identified myself as police and tried to open the driver's door, but it was locked.

I called Pete on the radio and asked where he was. He told me that the elevator to get down wasn't working. I then called the police radio to tell them we needed backup. At the same time, the male got the car started and was backing up to get out of the parking spot. I took out my 38 pistol and fired a shot at the driver's side tire (just like in the movies), but the car pulled out and headed east on Spring Garden Street. I radioed police radio and gave a description and a direction the car was headed.

Just then, Pete showed up, and we both jumped into my friend's Volkswagen to give pursuit but had a hard time starting it. We got a call from police radio that an automobile fitting the description was found parked in the 1500 block of Spring Garden Street with a flat tire. The car was recovered by its owner. Needless to say, the bad guys got away!

Police radio then asked me if there were any shots fired. I guess someone heard the shot and called the police. I informed the police radio that it might have been my Volkswagen backfiring.

In another instance, Pete and I were working the 10:00 a.m. to 6:00 p.m. tour and were at the apartments at 2200 and the Parkway, where there were reports of autos being stolen. We observed two males driving around the parking lot, watching them circle it several times. We parked Pete's car and entered the apartment building so the males wouldn't see us following them.

After a few minutes, the auto came around again, and this time, one male got out and walked up to a white Buick. Pete then left the building to get his car while I left the building and walked to the end of the parking lot. Pete radioed me that the male was already in the car. He had gotten it started and was leaving the lot. I pulled out my badge and yelled for him to stop. This time, however, the male increased his speed toward me. In response, I pulled out my 38 pistol and fired a shot at him, seeing it go through the windshield.

The car then turned left over the curb and went right around me. Pete pulled up in his car, and I jumped in. I called police radio to let them know we were in pursuit of a white Buick across Twenty-second and the Parkway. We were joined by uniformed patrol in pursuit of this automobile. After several blocks, the car turned right on Twenty-sixth Street. The guy stopped the car, got out, and placed his hands on the roof of the car. I patted him down and placed handcuffs on him. I asked him if he was shot because I noticed my bullet went right through the driver's side windshield. He said he didn't think so, but he did notice a hole in his shirt that wasn't there before.

We then looked inside the car and saw what appeared to be a bullet hole dead center of the driver's seat. The man was taken to CDD for processing, where he supposedly told the detectives that he stole the car for the windshield. I think he was trying to be funny, and he was happy to be alive.

Chapter 15

————◇————

UNIFORMED FEMALE POLICE OFFICERS

At the time I joined the Philadelphia Police Department, there were only a few female police officers in the department. Mostly, the female officers were attached to the juvenile aid division or JAD as the sex crime unit. All were plainclothes officers, not uniformed patrol.

During the late 1970s and early 1980s, the police department started hiring females for uniform street patrol. After graduating from the police academy, some went to work for the captains in the districts as clerks. Some worked in the operation rooms of the districts, and many went to uniformed street patrol and became fine police officers—moving up as they were promoted to corporals, sergeants, and higher ranks.

As rookie officers, they were paired with veteran male officers as they learned the ropes of uniformed patrol. When their three-month probation period was over, they were given their assigned patrol car, just as their male counterparts.

It took some time for the older, experienced police officers to feel comfortable around the female officers, but everything worked out just fine as it became more commonplace for the men to have female colleagues. As with the male officers, the females had unique personalities and problems, but everyone got along and did their job.

Because of the quota system for rank, some females were promoted to a higher rank and became supervisors. Most were very good supervisors or corporals, sergeants, and even lieutenants and captains. But there was one sergeant who was a very nice person and fine supervisor but who had one major problem. She was bred to eat! She spent most of her tour of duty stopping at delis and restaurants to dine. She even had her mouth wired to help her stop eating. We all felt bad for her. One day, she came to work and was holding roll call when her lieutenant asked her where her weapon was. It seems she came to work without her firearm.

She was then ordered to go home and get it. The only problem was instead of driving home in her personal car, she drove to North Philadelphia in her marked patrol—a great distance from her assigned patrol area. A captain from the Eighth District spotted her and called the Ninth District captain and asked why a Ninth District sergeant was in the Eighth District. Apologies were made and accepted.

One night, when she was working from 4:00 to 12:00 p.m., she stopped at one of her favorite eating spots and was there too long. Several uniformed officers decided to take the emergency lights off of the top of her patrol car. When she left the restaurant, she drove into the Ninth District headquarters, not realizing that her emergency lights were missing from her vehicle.

There was another female uniformed patrol sergeant who I came in contact with, who worked in the Fifth Police District. One night on the way home (I lived in the Fifth District), I observed four males sitting in an auto beside a 7-Eleven market. Knowing that some of these markets had been robbed in the past, I went to the nearest phone booth (there were no cell phones or pagers then) and called the Fifth District to ask for a uniformed backup to check the males out. That's when I met Sergeant Maureen Rush.

I identified myself as the Ninth District Burglary Detail and told them what I had observed. Sergeant Rush and I then checked the males out and ran a records check, only to find out that two of them had arrest warrants on them. They were taken to the northwest detectives division.

Years later, after leaving the burglary detail, when I joined the Narcotic Strike Force, Sergeant Rush was my supervisor—and a great supervisor she was! She soon was promoted to lieutenant. This lady was one hell of a cop. Later, after she retired, she became head of security at the University of Pennsylvania.

Chapter 16

─────◇─────

AFTER THE 9ᵀᴴ DISTRICT BURGLARY DETAIL

Sometime in early 1983, we had a change of command. We got a new captain and a new inspector. Both were a new breed of commanders that was being promoted through the police department. Instead of promoting from within the ranks of the Philadelphia police officers who had earned the right to be considered for these positions, even the police commissioner was now being picked from other cities and states.

Pete and I had seven different captains during our almost thirteen years on the burglary detail, and each one of those captains—along with different inspectors—kept us on the burglary detail because of our record. But we knew that the new captains and inspectors each had their own agenda.

Around the middle of March 1983, both burglary detail teams were called to the office of the new captain. When we went to see him, he told us that he was going to replace us because, as he said, we had been there long enough. We asked him if we did anything wrong. He told us no, it was just time for a change, and we should get our uniforms in order. When he got permission from police headquarters, we would be sent back to uniform patrol.

In all fairness, a captain has the right to pick his own burglary detail, but Pete and I—along with 9BD-2—had exceptional arrest records, and our past captains kept us for that reason. Our new captain, however, requested to the new inspector a change of burglary detail. The request was written up and sent to the police administration building/headquarters, where it was immediately turned down. The chief inspector, along with the police commissioners, said no to the captain's request, mainly because of our record, and saw no reason for a change. The new captain told us we would stay on the BD teams for now.

Pete was really happy, but I told him not to get too excited because as of July 1, at the start of the city's fiscal year, we would probably be back in uniform. I told him that was when all the inspectors and chief inspectors from the old school would be retiring, and the new ones would be in charge. I wish I had been wrong, but on July 4, Pete and I were back in uniform.

We were sent to our old squad in the Ninth District, Four-Squad. While standing roll call with our new sergeant and lieutenant, Pete and I, along with 9BD2, were given hospital details for a week. As described earlier in this book, hospital detail is the most boring detail in police work. It's where you have to sit outside a hospital room to guard a prisoner who was injured during an arrest.

It was obvious to us that hospital detail was some kind of punishment because those details are usually always covered by senior officers who request it or by rookies. It didn't take long to find out why we received that treatment, especially Pete and me. Come to find out, our new captain (Bman) was very good friends with the new captain of homicide, who a few years earlier was a lieutenant and who for some reason hated Pete and me. It had to do with an incident during the possible suicide attempt described earlier in chapter 8. When we responded to the call, the lieutenant told us to leave the area, only to be called back by him when the woman who was on top of a crane said she would only come down if I went up to get her. He disliked us, even more, when the story made the front page of the newspaper the next morning.

As the saying goes, "What goes around comes around." After a few weeks of the hospital details, Pete and I, along with the other BD team, finally got to go back on the street. I got back my old patrol car, #917. After a few months, Captain Bman was transferred, and we got another new captain. We knew this new captain from when he was a sergeant in the Ninth District. He knew about our work and asked Pete and me if we wanted to work for him as aides.

We decided to give it a try, but after a while, it was enough for me. I didn't like being his gofer, plus we got a new inspector from foot traffic who liked cowering down to the special officers. So I went back to being a street cop again in my old police cruiser #917. I had a new sergeant in charge of the upper end of the Ninth District, which was my end. His name was Richard Byrd, a Black gentleman who had been recently promoted. We got along great! If he needed certain areas covered in the upper end, he would always call for me on the 917 car. He knew my reputation and that he could always count on me. I hardly ever took sick leave and always saved my vacation time as long as possible.

A few years passed, and I continued making arrests and always had both sides of my patrol log filled with activity reports. Now all I was thinking about was finishing my years and getting to my retirement age.

I saw how the department had done almost a 360 from what it used to be. The districts even started a police officer of the month award to try to boost morale, but that didn't last long. While my activity warranted the award, I never received it, which was okay with me because I wouldn't have accepted it!

What Goes Around Comes Around

About a year after Captain Bman put Pete and me back in uniform, the man who practically raised me and who I loved very much passed away from colon cancer. His name was Joe Charles. Before he passed away, my best friend Jerry Farmer and I visited him at his mansion in Lafayette Hill, Pennsylvania. Joe told us he wanted his family to have an estate sale of the property and asked me to make sure his family received top dollar at the auction. I promised him I would.

The day of the estate auction, I noticed in the crowd our old Captain Bman with a lady friend. Everything he bid on, I outbid him, knowing that he would not let me outbid him further and that he would keep bidding higher. I only dropped out of the bidding when I knew he had paid too much for the item. Every item he bid on, I would also be placing a bid on that item, but it seemed we saved the best bidding for last. His lady friend was very interested in an oriental rug that came up for bid. The captain and I, as well as one other person, all bid on this rug. This other person that I happened to know was in the rug business. Every time the captain bid, I outbid him, then the third person bid higher. This went around a couple of times until the guy in the rug business dropped out, leaving only the captain and me.

I knew from working with Joe Charles just how much the rug was worth. The captain's lady friend really wanted the rug. By the time I dropped out of the bidding and let Captain Bman have the rug, he wound up paying $200 more than it retailed for. What goes around comes around.

Narcotics Strike Force

Around 1990, my sergeant, Richard Byrd, transferred to a new unit called the Narcotics Strike Force. The city had received funding to start this unit, and they were looking for officers to work it. Sergeant Byrd called me and asked me if I'd like to join the unit.

I told him I wasn't interested in working narcotics this late in my career, but he said he needed guys like me and that I'd like the change, so I put in for a transfer. Around this same time, I was learning to be a locksmith, so I'd have something to do when I retired in a couple of years.

I went to the strike force, which worked out of a trailer at the police academy. It was set up with only two shifts of work. The staff included a captain, four sergeants, and one lieutenant. We worked in the area where there were large sales of narcotics—sold by Jamaicans. It was a great operation, well-thought-out.

Arrests were made by filming narcotics sales then arresting the buyer several blocks away from where the narcotics were purchased, so the dealers didn't know about the arrests. After observing the buys and finally seeing where the Jamaicans kept the drugs hidden, at the end of the day, they closed in and arrested the dealers and confiscated the drugs.

It was still a small operation though, because the strike force had limited funding. Also, if you worked out of a trailer in the northeast section of the city, the needed paperwork was done at a local Police District—which only happened at the districts with cell blocks for both buyers and dealers.

An added complication was the fact that I was learning to be a locksmith from another locksmith shop—West Philadelphia Locksmith owned by Phil Paul. I had to leave his shop early to drive about an hour to get to the strike force headquarters, and it was wearing me down.

I bumped into a friend of mine, Steve Sacks, who I knew from when I lived at the Summit Park Apartments. He asked me how I'd been, and I explained to him what I was now doing. I told him I was working on a small operation, but it could be much better if the strike force had more funding and could expand the operation. It was then that Steve, who worked for ABC Channel 6, suggested a solution.

There was a show on Channel 6 on Saturday nights, he said, called *Prime Time of Our Lives* hosted by Gary Poppa (who has since passed away). Steve said he would talk to Gary about the strike force. I informed the captain of the strike force, who then went through the chain of command. Lo and behold, it was approved, and the operation was shown to *Prime Time*.

Shortly after that, the strike force got its own building in Germantown, along with patrol cars, cameras, electric typewriters, and extra staff to expand the size of the strike force. Being there were only two shifts, and now we had our own building, I was offered a job at building security. My hours would be from 11:00 p.m. to 7:00 a.m., which was great for me because I could go to the locksmith shop during the day to learn my new trade for when I retired in July 1992. It worked perfectly!

On my last day at the strike force, I started reminiscing about my years in the police department. I put my feelings on paper. A friend of mine, Rick Wilson, who performed and wrote songs, put my words to music in a song called "Yesterday, Today, and Tomorrow Too," a minor piece of work. In 1997, I had it copyrighted. See attached lyrics.

Yesterday, Today, and Tomorrow
(Rearrangement of "Yesterday, Today, and Tomorrow" from Porter
'92 and additional words by Wilson '92)

I've seen sorrow. I've seen joy
Kind of joy like a child with a brand-new toy
Oh, I felt the fear and satisfaction, too
Goes along with the job I do

Chorus:

You see, I've dedicated myself to helping others
Whatever job came in, you know that I'll come through
Just dedicating myself to helping others
Yesterday, today, and tomorrow, too
I've walked in rain and snow and the bright sunshine
Driven for hours and hours, didn't stop at any time
Oh, I've stood straight in a long parade line
Done a ton of paperwork, some of it not even mine

Chorus 2:

You see, I've dedicated myself to helping others
Whatever job comes in, you know that I came through
Just dedicating myself to helping others
Yesterday, today, and tomorrow, too
Doing it for me and you

Bridge:

Oh, oh, when it's over
And time for my gun and badge to retire
I'll think of those that lived this life of mine
And set their souls on fire
I've lost some family, friends, and brethren alike
Missed holidays and birthdays and all the other happy times

Well, I've fought smoke and fire just to save a life
Oh, sometimes had to take one
Left me with a lot of sleepless nights

Chorus 2

Chapter 17

―――⟨∾⟩―――

COMMENDATIONS
AND AWARDS

1. Merit
    Charges: Purse snatching, receiving stolen goods
    Date: 1/10/1971
    Award: Four Chaplins award from the citizens of Philadelphia
    Date: 5/23/1971
    Event: Fire rescue
    Date: 8/21/1971
    Charges: Aggravated robbery, aggravated assault, and battery
    Date: 7/24/1972
    Charges: Aggravated robbery, aggravated assault, battery, and other charges
    Date: 3/27/1973
    Charges: Purse snatching
    Date: 9/21/1973
    Charges: Multiple robberies, burglary, aggravated assaults, and weapons charges
    Date: 11/23/1973
    Charges: Strong-arm robbery
    Date: 3/26/1975
    Charges: Armed robbery, aggravated assault
    Date: 4/6/1977

Charges: Escaped prisoner armed felon
Date: 12/28/1980
Charges: Robbery, theft, and related charges
Date: 12/27/1973
Charges: Robbery and other related charges
Date: 2/27/1974
Charges: Robbery and other related charges
Date: 3/12/1974
Charges: Multiple counts of robbery, theft, and other related charges
Date: 5/22/1974
Charges: Robbery, theft, receiving stolen property, and conspiracy
Date: 8/15/1974
Charges: Purse snatch
Date: 9/27/1974
Charges: Attempted robbery and assault
Date: 3/16/1974
Charges: Rape, robbery, assault, and other charges
Date: 8/12/1975
Charges: Robbery, assault
Date: 10/23/1975
Charges: Two counts of robbery, one count of attempted robbery, simple assault, and other related charges
Date: 11/10/1975
Charges: Robbery, simple assault
Date: 4/27/1976
Charges: Robbery, theft, and related charges
Date: 4/22/1977
Charges: Robbery, conspiracy, and other related charges
Date: 12/14/1977
Charges: Robbery, kidnapping, and numerous other offenses
Date: 10/3/1978
Charges: Twenty-nine robberies and burglaries
Date: 12/16/1978 to 1/12/1979

2. Bravery
   Charges: Robbery, assault with intent to kill, and various other charges
   Date: 8/24/1972

My Pal Guido

Ever since I was a young child, I always wanted a horse-like most kids in our day. In 1986, I finally bought one. I went to Ashford Farms located in the Miquan section of Philadelphia. It was there that I found the horse I wanted. He was an 18 year old, but well trained Bay (Brown) in color. His name was Guido.

I boarded Guido at Courtesy Stables located in the Roxborough section of Philadelphia. Courtesy Stables was owned and operated by Earl and Valerie James. Earl was a retired Philadelphia Mounted Police Officer. Every Sunday, I would ride Guido from the stable to Valley Green Park, where I would buy a bottle of apple juice and a Honey and Oats granola bar for Guido. A little bit about Valley Green; it is located along the Wissahicken Creek in the Fairmont Park section of Philadelphia. There is a gravel and dirt road that runs for several miles along the creek, with a restaurant known as The Valley Green Inn right in the middle.

In 1929, the City closed the road to motor vehicles and named the road Forbidden Drive (no motor vehicles allowed). It became a major trail for riding horses, and horse carriages to travel—along with many pedestrians also enjoying the area. There were many horses and riders in the Valley during those days, along with Horse Shows at the nearby ring on Northwestern Avenue.

Every year for many years, the Park held the Wissahicken Day Parade—which was held on the last Sunday of April. Riders would come from miles around to be in this parade. Along with Horse and Carriages, prizes were the Ribbons that were given out. There were also Horse Shows for all different occasions. The first one we entered was for Halloween—where the horses and riders dressed in costume. I enlisted the help of my friend Jackie Simon, and we came up with a costume. We dressed Guido as a Chain Gang Prisoner wearing striped pajamas pants and I used my badge number "3026" as the prisoner number. I dressed as a Western Marshall, and we rode around the ring along with other contestants. We won the "Blue Ribbon", which is 1st place top prize. The next year we dressed him as Batman and again we took 1st place.

In May of 1997, our last parade was the Roxborough Memorial Day Parade. I led Guido along the parade route, with just a military saddle, a pair of cavalry boots attached to that saddle—facing backwards, in honor of deceased military during their funeral. I also wore a cavalry uniform. Our local newspaper put a picture of Guido and I on the front page of their Memorial Day Edition. That was an honor!

Sadly, on December 25, 1997– Christmas Day, Guido passed away. He was 28 years old. Needless to say, I was heartbroken—not to mention that it ruined that day for many people who knew Guido. My friend Earl James, upon my request, turned the rear bedroom in our home into what looks like a stable/tack room. It's a tribute to Guido, with his blankets hung and displayed on racks, as well as every saddle and parade costume and horse tack equipment. It is just like walking into a barn, with many pictures on display. Such great memories! I got permission from the Fairmount Park Commission to have a brass plaque placed on a bridge on the upper trail of the Wissahicken. The plaque reads "Guido's Bridge", a well-known and loved horse in the Wissahicken Valley, 12-25-97". That plaque is still there to this day.

Every December 25th– Christmas morning, before I do anything else, I go down to the bridge to reflect. I look at the Christmas wreaths and bows that are placed on the trees by the bridge. Also, next to Guido's plaque, I find a Christmas card from the Flickinger family. Next to the card is a paper plate with horse-shaped cookies wrapped in cellophane, made by their daughter.

P.S. I've never mounted a horse since. I think of Guido every day. Goodbye my friend, my pal, my horse. Forever, a million tears.

Chapter 18

IN MEMORIAM

Police Officers Who Died in the Line of Duty During My Twenty-three Years on the Job

Position	Name	Date of Death
Police Officer	Fredrick Cione	1/30/'70
Police Officer	Harry Davis	4/30/'70
Sergeant	Frank Von Colln	8/29/'70
Police Officer	John McEntee	2/20/'71
Police Officer	Joseph V. Kelly	2/21/'71
Detective	Douglas J. Alexander	2/9/'72
Police Officer	Leo P. Van Winkle	6/27/'72
Police Officer	James F. Duffin	1/14/'73
Police Officer	Louis J. Vasgar	4/13/'73
Police Officer	David F. Samson	12/12/'73
Sergeant	Michael S. Lingham	4/14/'74
Sergeant	William Kellehar	5/14/'74
Police Officer	James McHale	9/15/'74
Police Officer	Alan Lewin	4/10/'75
Police Officer	Ronald Trumbette	5/23/'75
Police Officer	Artemis Johnson	10/20/'75

Corporal	William L. Daniels	12/16/'75
Police Officer	John S. Trettin	2/29/'76
Police Officer	James E. Griffen Jr.	3/5/'76
Lieutenant	Walter L. Szwajkowski	6/27/'76
Police Officer	Francis W. Mago	3/30/'77
Police Officer	James J. Ramp	8/8/'78
Sergeant	Wilfred Doyle	12/21/'79
Police Officer	William Washington	1/16/'80
Police Officer	Ernest W. Davis	7/16/'80
Police Officer	Garrett T. Farrel	9/26/'80
Police Officer	James N. Mason	9/10/'81
Police Officer	Daniel J. Faulkner	12/9/'81
Police Officer	Sandra Griffen	2/13/'83
Police Officer	Stephen E. Sawka	6/18/'83
Police Officer	Richard Lendell	11/14/'83
Police Officer	John Duffy	12/10/'83
Police Officer	Thomas J. Trench	5/28/'85
Police Officer	Charles P. O'Hanlan	11/13/'85
Sergeant	Ralph Galdi	3/31/'86
Police Officer	Daniel Gleason	6/5/'86
Police Officer	William D. McCarthy	9/22/'87
Police Officer	Albert A. Valentino	10/23/'89
Police Officer	Freddie Dukes	12/25/'90
Police Officer	Winfield Hunter	6/4/'90
Police Officer	Joaquin "Jack" Montijo Jr.	6/14/'90
Police Officer	Daniel R. Boyle	2/6/'91

Robert M. Porter